The Thoughtful Caregiver:

Surviving, Thriving

And

Growing in Spirit

As You Care for Your Elderly Parent

Rebecca James Hecking

First Edition, 2016

ISBN-13: 978-1539611387

ISBN-10: 1539611388

In Loving Memory of my parents,

John and Dorothy James

And for the

Next generation of caregivers.

Contents

Introduction

I'm a car thief. Really. When my then 83-year-old father absolutely refused to stop driving, despite many attempts to reason with him, his doctor's orders and even his license being revoked by the state, I was forced to "steal" his car. With my stomach tied in a massive knot, my husband and I drove down to my parents' house, and I drove off with the car, leaving an explanatory note behind.

Afterwards, I stopped in a nearby parking lot where I promptly broke down into wrenching, whole-body sobs. I then drove the 100 miles back home. On the way, alone with my thoughts, I realized that something profound had shifted inside me. I was a different person on the drive home than I had been on the trip down. Later that evening, my father and I talked. He was angry, but eventually came to accept the new normal, albeit reluctantly.

Taking my dad's car was one of the hardest things I've ever done in my life. It meant standing up to someone who, despite his and my age, represented a major authority figure in my life.

It took courage and chutzpah. It signaled a shift not only in my relationship to him, but also a change within myself. That day in the car, the change was inchoate and foggy, but absolutely real.

Caregiving does that. It changes you. In the aftermath of Operation Car-Be-Gone (as we called it at the time), I found my heart opening with greater compassion toward my father who, after all, was losing his independence. Courage and compassion: that in a nutshell is the unexpected gift of thoughtful, mindful caregiving.

My caregiving experiences include three broken hips, two replacement knees, one dialysis emergency, dementia, diabetes, countless ER trips, two hospice placements, an open-heart surgery, low sugar, high potassium, anemia, at least a million pills and the occasional bout of gout. I have emptied a family home of a lifetime of possessions, then sold it. I am familiar with the organizational aspects of funerals and the virtues of various flower arrangements, coffins and urns. I have navigated Medicare and Medicaid, negotiated with banks and brokers, and sweet-talked grumpy neighbors. I have advocated on my parents' behalf with doctors, nurses, real estate agents, caregivers, administrators, auctioneers, aides, therapists, pastors and lawyers. I have cleaned up smelly messes. Did I mention that I'm an only child?

In short, I am all too familiar with the struggles of adult children as they face the trials and tribulations of caring for elderly loved ones because I have experienced them myself and lived to tell the tale. However, my story is not your story. By virtue of education and socioeconomic class, I experienced a level of privilege within "the system," and had an easier time navigating it than do many others who undertake this task with far fewer resources at their disposal. I am keenly aware of this, and have deep respect for all who face far greater challenges than my own.

When I was a caregiver, I found several excellent books on the nuts and bolts how of caring for an elderly relative, but nothing that really spoke to me personally as a caregiver, or that allowed me to reflect in a meaningful way on the overwhelming and powerful experience of caregiving itself. I have tried to write the book I wish I'd had when I was in the thick of it all. It is my hope that this book will be a companion for you as you face whatever challenges cross your path. I hope that you know you are not alone, even if you have moments when you feel that way. I also hope that if my own children ever find themselves tasked with caring for a stubborn and difficult elderly mother, that they will find something of value in these pages.

You can read this book straight through, or you can use the tag index to find chapters that speak to your specific needs. The chapters are loosely chronological, beginning with my initiation into caregiving, and ending with the time after my parents' deaths. Each chapter begins with a true story from my own experience The questions at the end of each chapter invite you to reflect more deeply on your own unique situation. These can be used for a journaling practice, or simply as food for thought. Caregiving can be a powerful life-changing catalyst for personal growth. You will be a different person at the end of it all. I guarantee it. I wish you all the best throughout your caregiving years and beyond.

Rebecca James Hecking

September 2016

Disclaimer: This book is focused on the personal experience of caregiving and is not intended as medical, psychological, legal or financial advice. I am not a medical doctor, psychologist, counselor, lawyer or financial advisor. If you find yourself in need of those services, you should seek out a professional who is qualified to offer appropriate information. The author is not responsible for any medical, legal or financial outcomes experienced by readers of this book.

Suddenly Caregiving

For me, caregiving began suddenly, with a phone call. I was in the Adirondacks in upstate New York, staying at a bed and breakfast while two of my kids were at camp. I was on a writer's retreat, working on the manuscript for my first book, The Sustainable Soul. That afternoon, I felt stuck and went out for a paddle on the lake with one of the free kayaks to clear my head.

Returning, I was stopped by the woman who ran the B&B. There was a call while I was out. My father had fallen and shattered his hip. He was in the hospital now, sedated, awaiting surgery the next morning. A flurry of phone calls and emails followed as we tried to figure out a plan. My husband was out of town, but my oldest son who was 16 at the time, was there with my mother for a visit, and was doing his best to help out and to comfort his grandma. He told me she seemed quite flustered by it all, but that he was doing his best to help her. The younger two were happily at camp, oblivious. It was Wednesday night, and the camp session wasn't over until Saturday morning. It was a two day journey by car from the remote wilderness where we were to my hometown where my parents still lived. There was just no way I could be there the next morning for the surgery.

We decided to let the kids finish their camp session. I would pick them up on Saturday and head back as quickly as I could. The next days felt like one long phone call as I talked to doctors, nurses, my mother, my husband, friends, other family and neighbors. I tried to work on writing, without success. So much for my writing retreat. Instead, I got some practical birthday shopping done that I knew would save me time later.

Most of all, I found myself spinning out scenarios in my head of the days to come. The fall was a bad one. The surgeon told me the break was one of the worst he'd ever seen, and dad's recovery would be long and slow, if he recovered at all. A few hours of Internet searching convinced me that dad would likely not survive for very long. He was 80. His health wasn't great. Now this. Mom would be alone. She would learn to be a widow. It would be hard, but she would be okay. Maybe we could get her an apartment near us.

At that time, I had no idea of the caregiving journey that would unfold over the next six years. Literally nothing of what I had imagined in my head those few days in the north woods actually happened. Reality turned out to be both better and worse than I had imagined. Mostly, I was just clueless.

Where are you in your caregiving? Chances are, you've been at it for at least a little while. People don't buy books like this one until it dawns on them that they will be caregiving for some time yet, and they'd better settle in and figure out how to cope. When did it begin for you? Was it gradual, like a slowly rising tide? Or sudden, like the whirlwind that I experienced? How are you coping? Steady as she goes, or hanging by a thread?

As I said in the introduction, caregiving will change you. You will be a different person at the end of it all than you are at the beginning, or even in the messy middle. If you choose to let it, caregiving can change you for the better. You will grow in compassion and kindness. You will have more empathy. If you allow it, your heart will be opened.

Mindful reflection on the process is what this book is about. Approaching caregiving mindfully, consciously, with awareness and intention can not only help you cope with the day to day struggles you will face, but it will also help you put your months or years in the trenches into perspective, leaving you with gifts that will be with you for the rest of your life.

If you are new to caregiving, know that it's okay to be clueless. It's okay not to know everything all at once. It takes time to figure out all the nuts and bolts of Medicare, Medicaid, assisted living, Meals-on-Wheels, Powers of Attorney, living wills, and the thousand other details that impact the lives of our elders. You will make mistakes, and that's okay too. You'll have bad days. Expect them. You will also have good days too, moments of pure grace and a few really good laughs if you allow them.

It's important to remember that you aren't the only one on the journey. Your parent is facing challenges too. It isn't easy to graciously cede control, endure one loss after another, and to accept help even if it is badly needed. Your own family will also change. Your caregiving will impact your spouse, your children, and any other family members involved with your loved one's care. The impact will be complicated, but it can be mostly positive when all is said and done.

Each person also brings his or her own baggage to the task. Unfinished business from years past as well as old resentments and issues may find a fresh airing, but the flip side is that everyone involved may grow closer as you face what the future holds. Approaching it all with mindfulness, openhearted honesty and love can only be a good thing.

Taking care of a loved elder, especially if that elder is your parent, is different than caring for a healthy child or a temporarily disabled spouse recovering from a surgery. Children grow up, most passing milestones and growing in strength, knowledge and autonomy. The end of your day-to-day parenting may be marked by a graduation, or maybe a wedding, but a joyful occasion to be sure. A temporarily ill spouse will recover, and your caregiving days will end. Maybe take a vacation to celebrate. But an elder? There are no growth charts, no happy milestones passed one after another, and no celebratory vacation when it's all over. The end of this journey is a funeral, which is its own sort of beginning as you navigate the choppy waters of grief and slowly process all that has happened. Of course we know this intellectually, but living it is another matter.

Wherever you are with your caregiving: clueless newcomer or seasoned veteran, take a deep breath. You are here, now, in this moment. The past is past, the future will unfold as it will. Take a deep breath. Take another. That's really all you have to do in the end.

Questions to consider:

- Did you imagine what caregiving would be like before you took on the task? How does reality compare with what you thought it would be like?
- What sort of support system do you have for yourself as you care for others? Who supports and cares for you?
- How do your challenges compare to those of your parent?

Tags: crisis, encouragement, planning ahead

Promises and Fantasies

I remember the day my mother gave me one of the greatest gifts I've ever received. She was in her late 60s, and my children were babies. The two of us were out for a walk with them on a sunny day when she was visiting. The conversation turned to memories of her own mother. She stopped in her tracks, turned to me and said, "I want you to remember something. If I ever get in a state where I can't care for myself, I want you to put me in a nursing home. Do you hear me? I mean it. Put me in a nursing home. I don't want you to even THINK of trying to care for me yourself." My twenty-something self was slightly insulted. Did she think I wouldn't do a good job? Did she think I didn't care? I mumbled something about not needing to worry about that for a really long time, then promptly changed the subject. Many years later, when she was suffering from dementia and a second broken hip in her 80s, I remembered those words with gratitude and love. I intend to say them to my own children someday.

My dad, on the other hand, would have none of this nonsense talk about ever needing a nursing home, or even assisted living. He never demanded promises from me, but he did entertain a lot of fantasies. Although he didn't expect me to move in with them full-time, he never really grasped how much effort and stress was involved even in part-time caregiving, and never EVER wanted to leave his home of fifty-plus years. According to him, their house was perfect, and they had everything they needed. No need to make any changes. Ever. According to him, he would die in that house. Everything was just fine.

I got really lucky in hindsight. I never made any promises to my parents about their care. Many loving adult children promise with complete sincerity and love that they will never put their parent in a nursing home. Usually, promises are made when the parent is relatively healthy and doing fine. Sometimes we make them voluntarily. Sometimes we are guilted into making them. Promises made about future care have a tendency to come back and bite us later in the game.

If you've already made such a promise to your parent, realize that you may or may not be able to keep it in the end. If you haven't made such a promise, then don't.

What kind of promises should we make? For several years, I participated in an online caregiver's discussion board. It was populated by many adult children wrestling with decisions about how best to care for their loved one without destroying themselves in the process. After a while on the board and with the input of many other users (especially one who went by the pseudonym of Grassflower), I came up with a statement that I frequently would repeat to my fellow caregivers.

The best care situation is one:

- that meets your loved ones physical needs

- keeps them as content as possible given their situation (note that this doesn't mean that they are happy all the time)
- allows you, the caregiver, to meet the other obligations in your life (children, work, etc...)
- AND does all this without wrecking your own health (physical and mental).

So looking at all that, what kind of promises can we realistically make? How about this: I love you and I'll do the best I can for you. We need to realize that our best can vary. My best on a day when I'm feeling great, the sky is sunny, work is going well, and little Johnny just brought home straight A's is a completely different thing than when I'm sick with the flu or there's a major problem at work. "Best" is relative, and we need to cut ourselves some slack. What's your best right at this moment? Are you over-reaching? Promising too much? Or are you doing reasonably okay juggling it all? Just do the best you can. You're doing fine.

Even if we never are put into a position of making promises to our elderly parent, we may be drawn into their fantasies. I don't mean unicorns dancing on rainbows. I mean the fantasy of being absolutely fine until one day you just sort of keel over, and die quickly and peacefully on the spot. That was my dad's fantasy. He would stay in his house forever, moving more slowly but still feeling fine, and then boom, lights out. Although occasionally this happens in real life, it's rare.

A local legend around here involves a retired professor who died while reading the newspaper in at the library of the college where he used to teach. Lots of our elders would wish for such a passing. More often than not, what plays out in real life is a slow dance of increasing disability, punctuated by various crises now and then. The level of care needed gradually grows over time. As adult children, we help our parents navigate this process.

Even if your parent lives in a fantasy world, you can't afford that luxury. Caregivers need to be firmly grounded in reality in order to do what must be done. We also need a keen awareness of our own limits: physical, mental, and psychological. Look back at the best care situation list above and compare it to the reality on the ground right now. Are you doing okay? How about your parent?

One persistent fantasy of adult child caregivers is that we can make our parents happy. The truth is that their happiness at any given moment probably has less to do with you than it does their personality and situation. Are they a glass-half full sort of person? Are they perpetually grouchy?

Circumstances may change, but basic personality doesn't. It's important to also realize that no matter how hard you try, you can't turn back time. Your parent is aging. No amount of smiley faced-sunshine and rainbows can change that fact.

So where does all this leave you? Only you can answer that question. Take some time and consider what promises you've made and what fantasies you and your loved one hold dear. Journal about them if you're the writing sort. No matter what, simply bringing promises and fantasies out into the light of day is a positive endeavor.

Questions to consider:

- Have you made promises to your parent? How do you feel about those promises? Were they made freely or did you feel coerced?
- Can you imagine a scenario where you would be forced to break a promise? What might happen then?
- How do you feel about your "best" being different from day to day? Do you judge yourself harshly or gently?

Tags: autonomy and control, denial, planning ahead, self-care

Black Sheep and Golden Children

I'll never forget when my mother's sister came to visit her in the nursing home. Mom had full-blown dementia at this point, her memory functioning for about five minutes on a good day. As my mom visited with her brother-in-law, I took my aunt back to see her room. Outside each room was a small curio cabinet. Families of residents were encouraged to fill it with personal photos and memorabilia. In my mom's cabinet I had placed several symbols of her earlier interests as well as a few very old photos.

As my aunt looked into the cabinet, she grew wistful as her eyes landed on my mother's high school senior portrait. "She always was the pretty one," she mused out loud, mostly to herself.

I was struck by how an adolescent issue came roaring back to life in a woman over 80. I felt sad for both my aunt and my mother, as I glimpsed a very old wound suddenly opened again after so many years. I felt my aunt's pain. I imagined them both as teenagers. I wasn't sure how to respond.

Looking back now, that exchange still amazes me. I am an only child, a situation that has its own advantages (no one to argue with) and disadvantages (no one to share the load) for caregiving. Clearly, the old issues were still very present for my aunt and my mother, and they clouded the relationship even after many decades of adult life.

Where are you in the constellation of your family of origin? Oldest? Middle child? Baby? Does your family have a black sheep? A rebel? A perfect, "golden" child? A quiet one? A quirky one? Did you get along with your siblings? Was your family generally functional or dysfunctional?

No matter what your situation, the dynamics of your family of origin will have an impact on your caregiving journey. You, and each of your siblings, have a unique relationship with each of your parents, for better or worse. Even parents who don't play favorites have relationships with their adult children that ebb and flow with time and circumstances. That's real life in loving families.

Who will do the lion's share of caregiving? Sometimes geography is the determining factor. The person who lives physically closest to the parent(s) often ends up doing most of caregiving.

Sometimes gender is a factor. It's an unfortunate reality that in the U.S., adult daughters end up shouldering a greater burden on average than sons. Frequently, these adult daughters end up sandwiched between generations, caring for parents as they simultaneously care for their own children. I don't mean to imply that there aren't also sons who step up to the plate and do the job too, but in many families, it ends up being the daughters more often than not.

Without a doubt, the best thing you can do to prevent conflict is open and honest communication among siblings. Cultivating trust in an atmosphere of mutual love and respect is key. Good communication can prevent the emergence of resentment, as the caregiving burden grows heavier with time. Nearby siblings need to speak openly, honestly and often to their far-flung brothers and sisters. Far-distant siblings need to respect the observations and judgment of the sibling closest to the situation. For example, it's not uncommon for the involved sibling to pick up on early signs of dementia that may not be evident to others who only speak by phone to the parent.

Your own role in your family of origin may influence how you approach caregiving. If you are the "dutiful one," you may feel obligated to take on more than you really should. If you are the black sheep, you may feel excluded and left out. Ideally, working with your siblings can help all of you to transcend old patterns and grow as individuals and as siblings as you face the challenge of caring for your parent together. Of course, reality doesn't always match the ideal.

Realize first and foremost that no relationship is perfect. You will likely have conflicts at some point with your siblings, but these don't have to escalate into all-out war. Expect it to be messy. Expect everyone to have to work at it. If you can manage to put yourself into your siblings' shoes and see the situation through their eyes, it can help to smooth the way a little bit, even if some major bumps remain. If communication seems awkward, consider a few sessions with a family therapist. Some therapists may be willing to work online through a group meeting video chat so that far-flung siblings can figure out how best to move forward. Having a compassionate neutral party involved can be helpful to defuse tension and to work toward meaningful solutions.

Be on the lookout for old patterns that may re-emerge as the situation with your elderly parent develops over time. Do you find yourself feeling like a five year old again? Do you tend to fall into arguments that feel like they've been recycled from decades earlier? Watch out for feelings like this, and bring them out into the open. Again, a skilled counselor can be helpful here. Even if you can't go as a group, consider a few sessions alone with a professional to help develop strategies to function as a healthy adult in whatever situations arise.

Of course, there may be times and situations where it is simply impossible for siblings to work together in any meaningful way. In such a case, sadly, legal help may be needed to sort it all out. You shouldn't have to sacrifice your own health and sanity to work with your siblings. In cases of extreme family dysfunction, prioritize your own well-being and seek counseling on your own as you navigate the situations that arise with your parent. If at all possible, leave the door open to future reconciliation as circumstances change.

Questions to consider:

- How does your relationship with your siblings influence the help and care given to your parent?
- Can you see any old patterns or scripts from your childhood repeating now as you care for your parent? How can you try to move beyond them?
- How can you foster good communication among your siblings so you can work together?
- What role (if any) do your and your sibling's spouses have in caring for their in-law parent? How does it impact the relationship among the siblings?

Tags: anger, autonomy and control, family dynamics, mindfulness

The Muffin Incident

What would become a mind-blowing, pivotal day in my caregiving years began like so many others. I was out for an ordinary weekly shopping trip, nothing special. Dad was at home, recuperating from his shattered hip. Mom and I headed off to the store.

There we were, wandering in the bread aisle. This wasn't a European-style, artisan-crafted, multi-grain bread aisle. It was a plastic wrapped, squishy sliced, bologna-sandwich bread aisle, which was the kind of bread my 50s era parents preferred. I had the list, and I told my mother to pick up a package of English muffins, whatever type she preferred. I turned away and went on to the next thing since she was standing directly in front of the muffins. When I came back a minute or so later, I found her staring blankly at shelves filled with exactly the item she wanted.

I asked her what was wrong, and she told me she couldn't find the muffins. I pointed to them, right there in her direct line of sight. She responded that she was looking for the words "English muffins" on the label (only the brand name was prominent, along with the muffins themselves visible through the plastic). I was stunned, and asked her again what she was looking for. She again told me. At the time, her Alzheimer's was not yet diagnosed.

She could read the list. She could walk the aisles of the store without a problem. She could see the actual muffins, the same type she'd eaten for decades, through the wrapper. She could read the brand name. But she didn't see the magic words, and that was what mattered. Her mind couldn't interpret the direct image of the literal, physical muffins themselves, or the other words on the package that could have hinted at the contents.

I felt myself become weak in the knees, with a punch-to-the-gut sensation. I grabbed on to the shopping cart to steady myself, and tried to take a deep breath. I mumbled some sort of response, grabbed the muffins and moved on. But inwardly, I was reeling. Something was terribly wrong.

Up until then, I had been in denial about my mother's cognitive issues. She had been having problems, but in the aftermath of dad's catastrophic fall, I chalked them up to a very understandable (surely temporary) depression. Or maybe anxiety. Or possibly stress. But certainly not dementia. Not Alzheimer's. No way. Impossible.

Up until then, her early-stage dementia was as invisible to me as the muffins were to her. I was staring right at it and just didn't see. The Muffin Incident as I've come to know it, lodged in my consciousness that day and has been with me ever since, floating around in my thoughts. It forced me to come face-to-face with my mother's reality, and by extension, the reality that she would need increasing care as time passed, and probably needed more immediate help than I had been willing to admit to myself.

Denial isn't always a bad thing. It is psychologically protective, and serves to shield us from things we might not be ready to handle. Looking back, I think that on some level, I realized that things weren't right, but until that day in the bread aisle, I hadn't been ready to face it.

Looking deeper, such experiences present the question of what is it that is right in front of us, but yet invisible? What do we really see? What other aspects of our lives are cloudy with denial? Where is denial helpful, and where is it problematic? Sometimes a little introspection will help us face those aspects of our lives that are dominated by denial. Other times, we might need to be whapped on the head with a proverbial muffin.

When we look at our world, do we see it as it is? As we wish it to be? Are we blinded by our own prior experiences? We all see the wider world through a lens of our own making, a filter of our own experience and prejudice. A few minutes on social media is enough to convince me of that. Is someone reasonable or radical? It might depend on whether or not they agree with me. Can I see past the label to the real thing? What exactly is the real thing?

What is it that is right in front of me, but yet invisible? What do I *not* see? What is the insight staring me in the face that still remains elusive? What blinds me? What holds me back? Considering this reminds me of the verse in the Christian scriptures where we are reminded not to fuss about the speck in another's eye while there is a log in our own. What a wonderful description of denial. We can clearly see how a close friend is in a dysfunctional relationship while any dysfunction in our own relationships remains hidden. We can clearly see the sibling dynamics between our cousins, but yet our own siblings are a mystery.

Realizing that like my mother, I am prone to trust my own preconceived notions, rather than the reality staring me in the face helps me to be a more compassionate person if I let it. It allows me to try to see through another's eyes. I can grow. My vision expands. I begin to remove the log.

Along your caregiving journey, there will be pivotal incidents for you like the Muffin Incident was for me. At the moment, you may be overwhelmed by immediate concerns, but as time passes, go back and look for the deeper, wider gift of insight that it offers. You will not be disappointed.

Questions to consider:

- Has there ever been a time in your life when you were in denial? How do you look back that time now?
- Is there an aspect of your parent's situation about which you are in denial? Are you ready to face it?
- Is there such a thing as healthy denial? How can denial serve you in a helpful way?

Tags: dementia, denial

A-Plusses and Deli Counter Deceptions

A&W diet root beer, canned sliced peaches, coffee (the one that's on sale), 3 bananas (maybe 4 but only if they're really small), Albert's Dutch loaf (not the other brand), exactly six slices of longhorn cheese (tell them to put the slicer on setting #4).

I won't bore you any longer with the rest of dad's grocery list. Trust me, it was very specific. I loved my dad, and I felt sorry for him. Physically, he was a shadow of his former self. He spent his days cooped up with mom, whose dementia was getting slowly worse although we hadn't quite faced it yet. He could no longer engage in his beloved hobby, woodworking. It was just too dangerous. So I tried to please him as much as I could with the small stuff.

"Did you get everything on the list?" he would ask when I got back to the car. If I answered with a yes, I got a smile and a nod, and I felt like I did when I was a kid and brought home a report card with lots of A's. Just like that little kid, I still basked in his approval. If I answered with a no, I got, "Well, why not?" and had to explain that they were out of this item or that. Sometimes, especially early on, at this point we would trek off to another store in hopes of finding exactly what he wanted. Usually store number two would have the item, but if they didn't, I would end up buying something else, and he would be grumpy for a little while, leaving me feeling like I'd brought home a D instead of an A. It was an exercise in frustration, and I found myself becoming more and more annoyed

every time it happened. One week when he was being especially grumpy and stubborn, and I was in a particularly lousy mood too, I deliberately bought the wrong brand of lunchmeat and didn't tell him. At the moment, it felt sneaky and good, but the next day I realized it was a wake-up call. Something had to give.

Shortly after dad's shattered hip, I began a pattern of weekly caregiving trips to my hometown, 100 miles from where I live now. I arranged my work schedule to drive down on Monday afternoon and return Tuesday morning. This would be our pattern for three years. By the time I deliberately bought the wrong lunchmeat, this routine was getting exhausting, physically and emotionally.

The following week, I started to just buy the other brand of whatever it was he wanted, rather than make the trip to the second store. I'd tell him so if he asked. Maybe I was just tired. I didn't need the A anymore. Maybe a C was okay.

Many of us (including me) were raised with the idea that it's a virtue to put ourselves and our own needs last, to run ourselves ragged in service to others. It has taken me a long time to un-learn that lesson, and frankly I'm still working on it. It's a twisted and unhealthy version of the Golden Rule, sort of a "do unto others" on steroids, with a heavy dose of guilt thrown in for good measure. I likely learned it from my mother, but I don't blame her for teaching me. After all, she was certainly taught by her mother and so on, back through generations of women, all taught to put themselves last.

Enough is enough. It's time we realize that our needs are just as valid and important as anyone else's, and that includes our elderly parents. There are times in our caregiving years when we are confronted with a choice of our own needs and those of our elders. I hereby give you permission to put your own needs on an equal footing with theirs. There will be times in your caregiving journey where you will be utterly spent, exhausted and at the end of your rope. At that point, you *need* to take a step back, rest, catch your breath. For an hour, a day, a weekend or whatever, you must prioritize your own needs. Pass the baton for the moment and care for yourself. Caregiving is a marathon, not a sprint, and you need to pace yourself, save your strength for the times when you really need it, not burn yourself out early on through neglect of your own basic needs.

It's also important to distinguish between needs and desires. I also hereby give you permission to put your *needs* ahead of your loved one's *desires.* When it came to shopping for dad, over time I realized that my need for sanity and getting the shopping done was more important than his desire for his favorite brand of diet root beer or longhorn cheese sliced just so. I wasn't going to be any good to him at all if I was so resentful and exhausted that I took out my frustrations through ridiculous deli-counter sabotage.

Your needs matter. Period. Taking care of your elderly parent is one of the most stressful and challenging things you will ever do in your lifetime, and putting yourself last is a recipe for burnout and resentment. It may be hard to let go of the mental image of your kid-self, A+ in hand, but for your own sanity, you must. You aren't a little kid anymore. The parent-child dynamic needs to evolve if you are to be the caregiver your parent needs you to be.

Not only should you prioritize your needs on an equal footing, you should actively give yourself a little luxury, a little pampering, in whatever form you like. Sip tea. Meditate. Take the exercise class. Get the pedicure on your day off. Buy yourself flowers now and then. Get the fancy flavored latte instead of the cheaper plain brewed cup. Nurture yourself. You deserve it, but more importantly, you need it. Little luxuries are like vaccines against resentment that will (I guarantee it) emerge if you allow yourself to run on empty for any length of time. Take care of yourself, and you will take better care of your loved one.

Questions to consider:

- What do you do to relax? You should have an easy answer to this question. If you don't, consider that a red flag.
- How often do you take time for yourself?
- If caregiving is a marathon, how are you pacing yourself? Are you doing too much?
- Consider needs vs. desires in light of both your parent and yourself. How are you prioritizing each?

Tags: anger, self-care, stress

Rotten Potatoes and Other Unpleasantries

Dementia. The word no one wants to hear. The nightmare scenario. It took many visits to the doctor and various tests over the course of months, but eventually the doctor said it out loud, the word I dreaded most of all. As it turned out, mom was further down the dementia road than I'd realized. Dad had been in denial for a very long time (I had only been in denial for a few months) excusing various lapses and unconsciously rationalizing mom's growing forgetfulness, but with him incapacitated from the broken hip, her forgetfulness and confusion were becoming clearer by the day.

Suddenly, things made sense. Mom couldn't remember me showing her how to pump gas only a week earlier. Dementia. She seemed incapable of understanding how and why to write a check to pay a bill. She thought dad's home caregivers were houseguests. Dementia. The spoiled fruit that had grown ten types of fuzz in the fridge? The bag of smelly rotten potatoes just sitting there by the back door? The 27 boxes of macaroni and cheese that they couldn't possibly use? The mood swings? All of it, all the crazy-goofy things that had been happening, the stuff I had chalked up to stress or anxiety, it all made perfect sense now.

I picked up the bag of potatoes, and some icky brown goo dripped on the floor below. Dammit. One more thing to clean up. Mom of course was astonished. How did the potatoes get there? Who put them there? Did the store sell her bad potatoes? Should we complain? Why weren't they put away where they belonged?

A half hour later, the potatoes were in the garbage, the floor was clean, and we were on to the next thing. What was that smell? Well of course she had taken a bath just yesterday. How could I even ask such a question?

Dementia is its own special type of hell. Let's just say that out loud. There are silver linings to this dark cloud, which we'll get to later, but they are few and far between. Dementia really is hell, sometimes for your parent and always for you.

Depending on the individual situation from day to day, your parent may or may not be upset or even aware of their dementia. One day things are fine; the next day is constant turmoil. There may be moments of blissful oblivion, where your parent inhabits a long ago, far away happy place, or there may be moments of severe disorientation that will be upsetting to experience. One day she is fully aware of her cognitive deficiencies; the next, he has absolutely no idea that anything is wrong at all.

For you, however, the situation is constant. There are no moments of happy ignorance for caregivers, especially for live-in caregivers, or caregivers whose loved ones are still hanging on and living alone in the family home. While it is absolutely critical for you to take a day or two away from your parent and your responsibilities to them on a regular basis, you also need to care for yourself in the midst of an ordinary caregiving day. You need a micro-break. Yes, I know. It sounds a little bit out there. Bear with me. Being physically present with a loved one suffering from dementia is emotionally exhausting, and there will be moments when you are at wit's end, and just can't take it another minute. You can't step out for an hour, much less a day, and you just can't face answering the same question your loved one has fixated on for that particular day for the hundredth time.

Is there a room in the house where you could just step in, shut the door and take literally three minutes to yourself? For some, it may be a spare bedroom, the laundry room, or the basement. It should be somewhere a little away from the thick of things. For some, the only place you've got is the bathroom. So be it. Wherever it is, this is now your sanctuary, your sacred space for three minutes.

What could you do for those minutes that would nurture your spirit? What would help you ground and center, come back to yourself, relax just a little? Look at the list below. What jumps out at you?

- A book of poetry
- A touchstone to hold
- Prayer beads
- A devotional book
- A small knitting or crochet project
- A bottle of scented hand lotion for a hand massage
- A small box of your favorite chocolates

- Aromatherapy spray
- A lump of clay to knead
- A rubber ball to bounce
- A small bell, singing bowl or chime to strike
- Something else, unique to you

Pick one or more from the list, put them in a small box or bag, and stash it in your sanctuary. Maybe you'll stash a book of poetry behind the towels in the bath. Maybe you'll keep some yarn and a crochet hook in the bottom drawer in the spare room. What you want is something that you can turn to quickly for a 3 minute break. Step into your sanctuary. Knit a row or two on a scarf. Read a poem. Take a few deep breaths. Savor a single chocolate. Massage your temples with your favorite lotion. Three minutes. That's all, but it can make all the difference in the world. You may have an outdoor sanctuary also, behind the rose bushes or next to the big oak tree perhaps, but you should have an indoor place as well that is available even on a rainy or cold day.

A dementia diagnosis requires a long-term care plan, not only for your elder, but for you too. How will you feed your soul for the duration of your caregiving years, however long they may be? How will you manage stress, and avoid burnout? How will you hold it all together? Well, you won't. Not all the time, anyway. You'll have moments when you utterly lose it, but you can help keep those moments to a minimum with a decent self-care plan, and that includes planning for micro-breaks. They are no substitute for full days away, or a week-long vacation, but they are a part of the bigger picture of self-care during your caregiving years.

Questions to consider:

- What was your worst caregiving moment ever? In hindsight, do you think that taking a break might have made it less awful?
- How can you build regular self-care into your life in a realistic and sustainable way?
- Are there specific ways that your parent "pushes your buttons"? Can you plan a strategy to deal with that predictable stressor when it occurs?

Tags: dementia, denial, planning ahead, rituals and traditions, self-care

Who Is This Person?

Alzheimer's-type dementia. That was the diagnosis. It was slowly sinking in for me at least, if not for mom. Dad, too, was finally saying the words out loud. Having an explanation for her bizarre behavior was helpful in an academic sort of way, but not much help on an emotional level.

The months that followed her diagnosis were filled with more weirdness, and at times I felt like I'd crossed over into another dimension, one where life was turned on its head and nothing was as it should be.

Once, when I was putting away laundry on one of my weekly caregiving trips, I discovered a bunch of bank envelopes tucked here and there in amongst the sweaters and socks. They all had money in them, mostly small bills. Looking around, I found dozens more, filled with ones and fives all totaling several thousand dollars. She must have been accumulating them for years to have so many individual envelopes, each with its little stash. Obviously, it wasn't a good idea to have so much loose cash just sitting there in the sock drawer, so I collected all the envelopes and gently showed them to mom, telling her that I would deposit all of it in her personal savings account, where the money would be safe and sound.

I expected, "oh my, how did those all get there?" followed by an agreement to put it all in the bank. What I got was a screaming tirade, very out of character. Mom ranted and raved, saying I could keep the money if I wanted it so badly. I was flabbergasted. I tried several times to explain, but no amount of reasoned logic could get through to her. The next day, when I deposited the money, she had forgotten all about it.

Another time, out of the blue while we were sitting watching the news, mom told me that when she died, I should be sure to take all the silverware out of the house immediately "so the people from the government won't come and take it," because apparently they do that. By now, I was as used to just sort of going along with whatever she said, so despite my doubts that the feds would swoop in with a salad fork SWAT team upon her demise, I promised her that yes, I would take it all home immediately and her silverware would be safe with me.

Who was this strange person and what had she done with my mom? It's incredibly difficult as an adult child to watch one's parent slip through the looking glass into another reality. It's also incredibly confusing to know what to say at any given moment. The response that worked yesterday doesn't work today. Should we try to correct them? Validate them? Gently draw them back to our world, or at least try?

Over time, and thanks to the good advice of some very kind strangers online, I adopted the go-with-the-flow approach to mom. Rather than try to get her to agree with my version of reality (the one where money is safest in the bank and where I do not fear for the butter knives), I joined her in hers, no matter how strange.

On the face of it, I did a lot of lying about weird tangents, small stuff, and inconsequential details that she would mix up and conflate, but also about people. When she asked for her own mother, I assured her that she was doing fine but was too busy to drop by today. What I came to realize is that for a person with dementia, the "truth" is whatever brings comfort in the moment. Harsh, black and white absolutely true-in-every-detail reality is not your friend. Fuzzy-edged, pillow-soft, gentle half-fiction is.

If your loved one's personality changes for the worse, the go-with-the-flow approach can help preserve some semblance of a positive relationship between you and your elderly parent. It's hard enough to endure watching a loved one slip away from reality. It's even harder to try to argue them back to your version of it, especially when all you get for your troubles is a barrage of angry words and hurt feelings.

Of course, the bigger question for you as a caregiver is coming to terms with the "new" version of your loved one. Often the new version is not pleasant or lovable. You may find yourself wrestling with some very big scary questions about your relationship with your loved one. If you are honest with yourself, and admit that you can't bring yourself to love what your parent has become, does that mean you don't love your parent? The more different your parent is now from how they used to be, the more it feels like you are interacting with a total stranger, the more likely you are to struggle in this area.

Going with the flow can certainly help mom or dad (and you) be happier in day-to-day life, but it is a very strange way to relate.

It may help to reframe the situation, to think about it a different way. Dementia and Alzheimer's disease are sometimes called the long goodbye. Truer words were never spoken. Your parent will leave you an inch at a time. There will be days where it seems like dad is really back. Savor those days. Other days, it will feel like his personality is completely gone. Survive those days. The day-to-day muddle can obscure the long story of what's really happening. How was dad six months ago? How was mom a year ago compared to how she is now? You can see the slipping away more clearly in this drawn-out view. The long goodbye will come into focus.

The questions that have to do with your relationship with the "new" parent are really the beginnings of grief. Losing a loved one an inch at a time means that you may grieve that way too. You may grieve the loss of your parent as you knew him or her. That grief is at the heart of the really uncomfortable issues involved with facing the new dementia-challenged version of the parent you once knew. It is a strange way to grieve. You see the person in front of you, clearly alive, but yet in so many ways, already gone, at least some of the time. So you half-grieve, or on bad days three-quarters grieve, but you can't grieve fully because, well, there they are looking back at you. So you go with the flow. You muddle. You do the best you can.

At the end of the day, it helps to just own the whole big ball of weirdness for what it is. Painful. Bizarre. Tragic. Unsettling.

Uncomfortable. Heartbreaking. Challenging in ways you hadn't even imagined. As my kids used to say, you're on the struggle bus now.

There you are in the thick of it. Step back, and see yourself in the middle of it all, hanging in there the best you can. Look at you, coping, adapting, going with the flow, making it up as you go along...look at you, brave soul. You will get through it. Give yourself a pat on the back. Your mom would be proud. Trust me on this one.

Questions to consider:

- What does love mean in the context of a relationship with someone with Alzheimer's?
- How does your relationship with your parent right now compare to that relationship a decade ago? Is it generally better, worse, or just different?
- How is it different to grieve a sudden loss versus the inch-by-inch losses from dementia?
- Have you changed as a result of your caregiving? If so, how?

Tags: comfort, dementia, encouragement, grief, through their eyes

Stories from the Neighbors

Gradually, I was getting a handle on the situation. Mom had dementia. Dad was in denial about that, and physically pretty shaky himself. The overall situation was precarious at best. Over the next few months, I would hear stories from concerned neighbors and friends that confirmed my suspicions about how bad things really were. One neighbor told me of several falls: sometimes dad, sometimes mom. He would come over and help pick them up from the floor or the grass. A church friend warned me about dad's driving. The mail carrier told me she had tried to keep an eye on them because she was worried. I gave her my phone number. I gave everybody my phone number.

One Monday afternoon, as I was walking into the house, dad called out to me, "I don't want you to worry. It's not as bad as it looks." Two seconds later I walked into the living room to see mom, with two black eyes from a flat-on-the-face fall in the driveway the day before. Off to the ER we went despite objections all around. Of course, mom had no recollection of how she wound up looking like a raccoon and was shocked every time she passed a mirror.

It was becoming clear that the picture they tried to present to me (doing just FINE thank you very much, no need to worry) was not exactly accurate. What else did I not know? If I asked them a very specific question, something like, "did mom fall on the patio last Tuesday?" they (or more accurately, he) would answer, but more often than not, the story was fragmented. There was an awful lot they simply didn't tell me. For mom, the dementia was the reason, but for dad, his answer was always that I was busy and did so much already, and he didn't want to bother me.

From their point of view, on the face of it, they really didn't want to bother me. Deep down, I think dad also knew that being honest with me would mean being honest with himself about the reality of the situation. Denial was preferable to confronting the way things really were.

As an adult child caregiver, it is very easy to be complicit in this sort of denial. We too might not really want to see things as they really are. The danger of that mindset is that in not acknowledging reality, we don't prepare for the inevitable changes to come.

Once when I was discussing dad's health with a hospital nurse, she said to me, "You're living in reality. Most people aren't." I've often remembered those words for issues beyond physical health and they've stuck with me. What is your reality? Are you living in it?

That's not quite as easy a question to answer as you might think. The rosy-glasses crowd may live in denial, refusing to see a deteriorating situation. On the other hand, pessimists with imagination tend to spin out worst case scenarios and ruminate on them, and wind up anxious and depressed. Reality is usually somewhere in between. Reality is messy and muddy and full of uncertainty. Reality is complicated. It's almost never as bad as you fear, but never as good as you hope for either.

Living in reality means that we don't have clear-cut certainty. We deal in probabilities and risk-assessment. It also means we need to become comfortable not only with our own tolerance for risk, but with our parent's tolerance as well. As adult children, we often want 100% safety for our parents. If we're honest (and living in reality, we absolutely should be), we want this as much for our own sake as for theirs. If they are in a safe environment, we are less likely to get the dreaded middle-of-the-night call requiring us to turn our lives upside down to deal with a crisis. Our tolerance for risk tends to be less than that of our parents, who often prefer personal autonomy over safety. Their acceptance of risk is much higher than our own, and they may not fully realize the impact of their decision on others, including you.

As long as your parent is cognitively intact, living in reality means taking both perspectives into account and trying to come up with a plan together. Can you both compromise a little? It's easier said than done.

So how can you live in reality when your mom or dad is as stubborn as a mule, refusing to acknowledge very real risk, refusing to give an inch, and absolutely refusing any sort of change whatsoever? On a physical level, it means getting an accurate picture of the situation as it really is. Seek out neighbors, friends, and any who come in regular contact with your parent. Ask them what they see, and then start to make some real on-the-ground backup plans based on your reality. This can mean standing up for yourself, your limits and your needs, and factoring them into your broader plans. Living in reality means that your loved one's physical needs and tolerance for risk are managed in a way that allows you to have some measure of peace and stability in your own life.

Living in reality on an emotional level is something else entirely. It involves confronting our own feelings about the situation as it is. Acknowledging our own resentment, frustration, anger, and sadness helps us see beyond them. If we can own these feelings, even the ugly ones, we can begin to open our hearts in spite of them, and cultivate genuine empathy for our loved one and compassion for ourselves. This too is easier said than done, and requires us to circle back, again and again, to an acknowledgement of our own and our parent's feelings, and to refuse to let ourselves slip into bitterness. Balancing open-hearted empathy and care toward our parents with a healthy dose of self-love and respect for our own limits is an ongoing process, but it is this process that leads to personal growth over time even in the midst of our caregiving years.

Living in reality is a balancing act. We balance the absolute needs and personal wishes of our loved ones with our own needs and wishes, all with our eyes (and hearts) wide open. This is something that is never really "achieved" in a permanent way. It's an ongoing process. Reality is like that.

Questions to consider:

- Fess up. Are you living in the reality of your situation? If not, do you tend toward the rosy-glasses end of the spectrum or the doom and gloom end?
- What is the state of your emotional reality right now? Are you stuffing down any unpleasant feelings or acknowledging them?
- How are you balancing the many aspects of your caregiving situation? Are some factors weighted more heavily than others?

Tags: autonomy and control, denial, planning ahead, through their eyes

The Endless Parade

It was becoming abundantly clear that mom and dad could not manage on their own. Mom's dementia had gotten to the point that she was at risk of burning down the house in any number of ways. An untended pot could quickly become a hazard, and I'd pulled out the equivalent of a small sheep from the dryer lint collector that she'd forgotten to empty. Dad was physically incapable of filling the gap. He was unsteady on his feet and needed a walker full-time now.

We'd had professional caregivers briefly following dad's hip break, but I had assumed at the time that they would help out for a couple weeks at most. Now it was obvious that we needed them back on a more permanent basis.

Of course, there were a million questions. What could we afford? Would we hire through an agency or privately? Agencies screen their employees and can always send someone in a pinch, but they are more expensive than a private hire and have strict rules about allowed duties. Privately hiring meant there were fewer restrictions, but more work for me in terms of paperwork and taxes.

It also meant that if the person didn't show up one day, that there was no one available for backup. What did I expect them to do? How often would they come?

Eventually, we settled on hiring through an agency: one person, every day for two hours to cook dinner, do laundry, clean, and attempt some personal care with mom. With so much to do and so little time, dinners would have to be pretty basic. Cleaning would focus on the most critical areas, like the bathroom. Unnecessary tasks like ironing would simply be dropped. I would also pitch in on my weekly overnight trips.

The workers themselves were a mixed bag. Most were older women a few years away from their own retirement. Most were kind and did an adequate job. A few were absolute angels, going above and beyond. We had one bad apple, caught rummaging through a desk where she had no business being. She was promptly fired. After a few months getting the bugs worked out, we all adjusted to the new normal: an endless parade of strangers, coming and going every day just to maintain the fragile status quo.

Inviting paid help into the home does solve some problems. It lightens your load as primary caregiver, freeing you up to focus on the more complicated tasks like handling medical appointments or managing finances. If you aren't local to your parent, it also provides a daily check-in, a set of eyes that can, ideally, provide you with some useful insights.

Paid help is also a luxury that many cannot afford, and it is far from a panacea for every situation. Perhaps the most difficult part for both you and your elderly parent is the intimacy of the situation. A tremendous amount of trust is needed to allow a stranger into every room of the home, every aspect of life, especially if the help involves such personal tasks as bathing and dressing. It can be unsettling for your parent when things aren't done the way they've always been done. Even little things like where a favorite coffee mug is stored, or how to cook scrambled eggs can seem huge.

For you (and for your parent too), the inner work involved here centers around control. Once you have hired people you believe are trustworthy, you need to step back and let them do their job. It doesn't help your stress level if you go back and re-do what the paid help just did, just because they did it a little differently than you would. Of course, letting go is easier said than done. It can help to spend some time examining your feelings about control in general. How much control do you need over situations in your own life? Are you detail oriented or laid-back and relaxed?

Bringing in paid help also acknowledges that you actually *need* that help. This too brings up issues of control. For many people, simply admitting that a situation has become unsustainable, and that they need help, is perceived as a failure. Let me say this loudly and clearly: you are absolutely NOT a failure if you cannot manage to care for your parents completely on your own.

Think of a nursing home. How many people are needed to keep it going? A typical nursing home employs nurses, aides, cooks and other kitchen staff, janitorial staff, activity directors, psychologists, pastors, administrators, financial managers, physical therapists, occupational therapists, and a host of volunteers. Many of these positions are staffed 24-7, requiring three shifts of workers every day. If you, the adult child caregiver, are attempting to manage this all on your own, you are doing the work of all these people combined! There is no shame in seeking out paid help if you can afford it. Cut yourself a whole lot of slack here and relax.

Finally, bringing in help can result in a lot of guilt heaped on you, the adult child. Your parent may not welcome these strangers, no matter how necessary their presence may be, and they may take out that frustration on the safe target, namely you. They too are struggling with issues of control. Paid help in the home is a signal to your loved one that they are no longer fully in control of their own home, much less the details of their own life. Recognizing this frustration for what it is can help take the sting out of complaints and criticisms that may be tossed your way, even as you struggle to do the best for your parent.

Eventually, the endless parade of caregivers may not be enough to adequately do the job. Recognizing the temporary nature of the arrangement can provide some perspective. Life for your parent (and you) is changing, sometimes quickly in a crisis, sometimes slowly, but change is the norm, regardless of how we feel about that fact. Acceptance of change and loss of control: these are the root issues of much of the caregiver's journey.

Questions to consider:

- How do you and your parent experience issues of autonomy and control differently?
- How has this changed over the course of your caregiving experience?
- Where is your parent on the spectrum between full independence and complete helplessness? How have the changes you've already experienced affect your relationship?

Tags: autonomy and control, family dynamics, systems and structures

Parent or Child?

"So, how was she this week?" I would ask after the waitress left with our order. Dad and I had taken to going out to an early breakfast on Tuesdays before I had to leave for home. Mom was sound asleep and would stay that way for several more hours at least. We always left a note on the mirror just in case. It was a calculated risk to leave her for an hour, but for dad, these brief moments out, along with the chance to speak freely were a lifeline.

We had a favorite restaurant, and he ordered the same thing every time (fried eggs, bacon, home fries, toast) to the point that our regular waitress stopped even asking what he wanted. She only looked at me, since I was the fickle one: oatmeal one week, eggs the next. They always sat us at the first booth, the one closest to the door. It was a little easier for dad to navigate with his walker. I was grateful for the small kindness.

So how was she this week? He would launch into a description of the latest issue. Maybe he tried to get her to bathe, and she refused. Maybe she thought the caregivers shouldn't be allowed into the kitchen. Maybe she got angry at him for some perceived insult. It could be anything. Mostly I listened for a while, then we would attempt a little brainstorming. Dad was a problem solver, and trying to come up with strategies to deal with what was really an impossible situation at least gave him some feeling of control in a situation that was slowly spiraling out of control.

Sometime during these months it occurred to me that there had been a shift in my relationship with mom. In many ways, she was the child now. Dad and I were the parents, loving and worried, wanting the best for her. It would be another year before I experienced that same shift with dad, becoming a "single parent" to both of them in the process.

When you're a child, you are in the care of another, usually a parent. You are fed, bathed, clothed, and taken to the doctor when you are sick. Assuming a normal, healthy situation, your basic physical needs are met without you having to think about it or ask. Hopefully, your emotional needs are met as well. You are comforted when sad, given encouraging hugs when you need them, and protected from what you aren't able to handle emotionally.

At some point in your caregiving years, the dynamic of parent and child may flip, especially if your parent has dementia. You no longer look to your parent for emotional support, validation and encouragement; he or she now looks to you. Realizing this can leave you feeling quite unsettled. For those of us who had "good enough" parents, who were loved and cared for, this shift can feel like a loss to be grieved, and it is. No one will ever love us quite the way our parents did. Parental love, even when complicated and less than ideal, is less conditional than other loves we may experience in our lives.

The realization that the parent/child dynamic has shifted may occur to you suddenly, or it may dawn on you gradually over many months, only to be recognized in hindsight. Often it occurs when you realize that your parents look to you for guidance instead of the other way around. They trust you to take care of them now, and you are suddenly aware of this trust. In any case, it is a major change in your relationship with your parent, and deserves to be thoughtfully acknowledged.

It is a loss for us, the adult children. Even as our parents begin to decline physically and possibly mentally, there is always a little part of us that believes (even unconsciously) in the possibility of going home again. If my life falls apart, mom won't turn me away. If I need it, dad will help me. Perhaps you actually *did* return back to the nest as an adult, after a job loss, divorce, or illness. Maybe you only held the possibility as an option in the absolute worst-case scenario imaginable. Maybe you never gave it much thought. In any case, when the dynamic shifts, the reality is that we really and truly can't go home anymore. Mom and Dad can't take care of us anymore. That is a loss that we must grieve, along with the loss of the parent/child relationship itself. If our relationship with our parent has been bumpy or less than we needed growing up, grief can wash over us for the loss of possibility. If you have shifted into the parent role, emotionally and/or physically, for your own parent, you lose the possibility of ever experiencing the parenting you may have wished for your whole life. Grief over the loss of possibility is real grief, no less significant or genuine than grief over any other loss.

Allow yourself to feel what you need to feel, and to process your emotions slowly and mindfully. Vent to a trusted friend, or to your journal. Cry as much and as often as you need to cry. There are no clear paths here, no direct route from being in the role of adult child to being in the role of parenting your parent.

The upside, such as it is, is a chance for some genuine emotional growth on our part. Parenting our parent is a chance to really, truly grow up, to become responsible for our own lives, our own emotions, our own spiritual direction. It's time to let go of blaming our parents for their shortcomings when we were children. It's time to let go of the need for validation from them. It's time to let go of old hurts and resentments. It really is time to grow up. It's time to step into our own fully adult selves, to step into who we are becoming: real, honest-to-god grown-ups able to face the world one day at a time, with as much grace and dignity as we can muster. It's time to learn to care for ourselves, to mother and father ourselves, to become grounded and centered enough that our validation of who we are comes from within, not from an external source.

The roles have flipped. The parent is the child. The child is the parent. Nothing will be the same from now on, and that's okay.

Questions to consider:

- Have you experienced the parent/child shift yet? If you haven't, can you see it coming on the horizon?
- Spend some time considering your parents as people, not just as your parents. What were some of the defining issues of their lives? How do those issues shape the people they are now?
- How can you begin to "parent" yourself in a healthy way, to show yourself unconditional love and support as the adult you now are?

Tags: autonomy and control, family dynamics, grief

Holidays

"I don't know where they are! They've got to be here somewhere! Didn't you pack them??"

"Maybe we left them at home. Better go back."

"I've searched the whole house. I can't find them."

"They aren't in the car."

"You did write them out, didn't you??"

The Christmas cards (the ones with money for the kids) had gone missing. Or maybe not. Maybe mom had signed them and put the gift money in, or maybe not. They could have been in the suitcases, in the car, in her purse, left at home on the desk, or even left in the refrigerator next to the butter for all I knew. For about half an hour, we searched. We were already late even before we went back to try to find the cards.

In the end, we gave up and drove two hours straight north to the town where I live. All the while, I tried to breathe deeply and calm both myself and them down as the back-and-forth squabble over the cards' whereabouts continued for miles. The cards (if they existed at all) were never found. All this drama took place just a few days before Christmas, which is not exactly a stress-free time of year.

At this point, mom's dementia was becoming more obvious, but hadn't yet reached crisis levels. Mostly, this period of time was marked with frustration and confusion for all, with lots of little daily details becoming lost in a fog of fading memory.

I think they enjoyed Christmas that year. They stayed at a motel since neither could navigate the stairs to our second floor guest room anymore. We had the usual big fancy meal on Christmas Eve, and opened presents together on Christmas morning. There was also an awful lot of napping in chairs, trying not to crash the tree with dad's walker, and frequent questions from mom, "What are we doing now? When are we leaving? Where are we going?"

I'm a big fan of simplifying the holidays. We observe our family traditions and we do give gifts, but we try to focus on enjoying time together and not get too caught up in commercialism. Even with a healthy mindset, the holiday season can still become stressful. Different branches of the family may have different ideas about how, when, and where to celebrate. Trying to meet the needs of small children and fragile elders gathered under one roof (possibly yours) can stretch patience to the limit. Old hurts and resentments tend to bubble to the surface again, and sibling rivalries that are decades old get a fresh airing.

An added stressor is the thought that maybe this might be your loved one's *last* holiday season ever. Of course, no one ever knows for certain, but for caregivers of frail elders, it's completely normal to have this thought cross your mind throughout the season. It adds a lot of pressure to have an extra special, extra loving, extra perfect (HA!) holiday. It also adds extra headaches and extra stress.

I've written elsewhere in this book about the need to let go, for the sake of both for our loved ones and ourselves. At the holidays, letting go can be especially difficult but also necessary. We need to let go of the mythic perfect holiday as a goal, adjust to reality, and simplify accordingly.

For elders, simplifying may come as a relief. They too may find all the seasonal hoopla exhausting and overblown, and if dementia is a factor, holidays can be especially confusing. Elders may be expected to interact with family members whom they rarely see, and children who have grown so much they are barely recognizable. On top of that, they may be introduced to new babies, or cousin Ed's fiancée, or Aunt Jane's new in-laws, all of whom they have never met. For an elder who is a little foggy on the best of days, this may just be too much.

So, simplify both your schedule and your loved one's. Drop anything that you don't enjoy. Build in extra downtime for your parent (and you). Politely decline one-too-many invitations. Call the caterer or get take-out instead of cooking it all yourself. Delegate duties to other family members. Do all those things. Yes, do.

And then, make sure that in all your simplifying, you don't let go of the *one thing* that is most meaningful to you this time of year. What is it? How can you make it happen in spite of the challenges of caregiving? Simplify the busy-ness but hold on to what is most meaningful and special about the season.

And then...Take a deep breath and let go of the whole added "last holiday maybe" pressure. The truth is that we don't know when or how our mom or dad will eventually die. The truth is that we don't know when or how *any of us* will eventually die. No matter how much control we think (or wish) we have over our lives, no matter how frail our parent may be, no matter how sure we are, issues like last-holiday-maybe usually fall into the category of the unknown.

When you find your mind drifting into last-holiday-maybe territory, take it as a signal from your unconscious to mindfully pause and be fully present in the moment. Remind yourself that the future is a mystery, and the past is past. Create a mantra for the season, and repeat it slowly in your mind to call yourself back to the present. Create personal rituals just for the holidays that ground you and help you stay calm. Something as simple as a nightly cup of tea can become a calming ritual if it is done mindfully and with intention. Begin it at Thanksgiving (or earlier if you like), and make it a daily habit through New Years Day, Twelfth Night or whatever date suits you.

Eventually, in hindsight, you will have had that last holiday with your parent. But between now and that day, embrace the mystery and sacredness of the moment.

Questions to consider:

- What is the one tradition that you absolutely must do no matter what? How can you adjust other things to make sure it happens?
- Conversely, how can you simplify both your and your parent's holiday? What can you drop that would make your life (and your parent's) easier?
- What are your parent's physical and mental limits right now? How can you respect those limits?

Tags: dementia, mindfulness, stress

Finding the Humor

It was a normal busy Monday. I'd arrived at my parents' home with a to-do list a mile long. At the top of the list was a haircut for mom. I would drop her off at the hairdresser and pick her up an hour later. I had promised her an ice cream cone afterwards.

We were finally on our way after the usual half hour prep required to take mom out of the house: dressed appropriately, bathroom stop, find her purse (no money, but no matter), shoes on, laces tied, coat on, down the stairs we go very slowly and carefully (she adamantly refused to use the chair lift we had installed a few months earlier), coat off, another bathroom stop, coat back on, find the cane, find the purse again, annnddd into the car we go. Whew!

I had pulled up to an intersection, when suddenly as the light turned green, another car quickly approached us from behind, zoomed ahead and cut us off. I narrowly missed a fender-bender. Catching my breath, mom declared, "Did you see what he did? I'd give him the finger if I could remember which finger to give!!"

After a stunned pause, we looked at each other and cracked up, loudly. After the appointment, I made sure to get her that ice cream. That day, she really earned it.

Over a year later, in the nursing home during a "false alarm" when we thought she might not make it through the night, mom (hooked up to oxygen) looked over at me smiling and said, "I'm still breathing!" then laughed out loud at herself. Her humor, if not her mind, stayed intact until the very end, and she taught me how to laugh when I felt like crying.

There are moments in your caregiving journey where you can either laugh or cry. Always choose to laugh. The incident above occurred when mom's dementia was really taking hold, and it was becoming more and more difficult to take her out of the house. I was wondering how much longer the hair appointments would work, but on that day, we both found something to laugh about.

The topics in this book are generally not very funny. Nursing homes, hospice, dementia, decline... nothing very funny about any of it, but even in the middle of the most difficult days there are moments of grace and humor. Choose to embrace them!

For most of my caregiving years, I took part in an online discussion group for dementia caregivers. There was one thread that always got heavy traffic. In it, people posted the humorous things their loved ones said or did, or shared situations that reflected the absurdity of it all. The humor was very much an "in group" sort of thing, stuff that none of us would *ever* say to anyone not familiar with dementia, sort of like how cancer patients can make the sort of dark jokes about cancer among themselves that would be horribly offensive if said by anyone else.

A support group can be a lifeline, especially for sharing a little levity. If at all possible, you should find one either online or in person. An online group lacks the face-to-face closeness of an in person local group, but the anonymity can be very freeing. You can complain and rant to your heart's delight, as well as share the funny stuff, in a community of people who really truly *get it.*

Especially if your parent suffers from any form of dementia, it's really important to find laughter together. Dementia sufferers tend to pick up on the mood of those around them, and mirror it back. In practice, this means that if you are in Debbie Downer mode every time you are with them, they will pick up on that mood and feel down themselves, which of course only makes it worse for you. By contrast, if you can share some humor about your day, or just life in general, you can laugh together. You can also reminisce, and share the humor of decades past. Depending on the progression of dementia, your parent may still have excellent recall of events from your childhood, or their own youth.

One of the (very few) good things about dementia is that in many ways, it gives you, the caregiver, a reset button. If you really screw up one day, chances are the next time you see your parent, they will have forgotten all about it. The reset button was pushed. The slate is clean. All is well. The trick, of course, is that YOU must let go and start fresh too. Can you laugh it off? Find the humor and keep going? It's worth it to make the attempt.

Humor can sometimes be a way to connect with a little bit of your parent's personality before dementia took hold. I'm sure there's a very scientific neurological explanation, but every once in a while, it's as though the old personality breaks through the fog of dementia.

You may have moments when you feel like your "real dad" made an appearance again. Savor them.

The flip side is that as dementia progresses, and your parent's personality changes, that the "new" version (Mom 2.0) may actually be funnier and less restrained by social norms than the original. If this is the case, then just enjoy it as a rare silver lining and don't feel guilty about that enjoyment. Do expect the occasional inappropriate remark, and just roll with it. One thing dementia can do is to remove some of the filters that we use to navigate social norms. Up to a point, this can be good. If, on the other hand, the changes move beyond the funny and into the truly offensive and inappropriate, you may need to limit or carefully manage your parent's public outings. Few people are sympathetic to an elder who is behaving badly in public (or to their caregiver).

However dark the road is, however difficult things are, be open to random splashes of humor. Laugh every chance you get.

Questions to consider:

- Have you had any funny moments in your caregiving journey? Share one with someone, either online or in person.
- Is your parent generally a serious person or the type who was the class clown in younger years? Have they changed over the decades? How?

Tags: comfort, dementia, encouragement

Out of the Blue

It was an ordinary weekly caregiving trip. I had shopped for the groceries, put gas in the car, and taken mom and dad to the doctor's. We decided to go out for dinner. I parked in the handicapped spot: a nice, level spot with dry pavement, and lots of room to maneuver. I helped dad out of the car and gave him his walker, but while I was doing that, mom started to get out of the back seat.

"Hold on a minute, I'll help you."

"I'm fine. You help your dad."

"No, you wait. Just give me a second..."

And then it happened. On dry level pavement, on a sunny day, with no obstacles in sight, mom suddenly lost her balance and did a twirly full-circle move, like a drunken ballerina. Before I could get to the other side of the car, she was down. Dammit, mom...

The restaurant manager rushed out, having seen the whole thing. He was in full panic mode, offering to call an ambulance. Mom insisted that she could get in the car, and with help, she did. Knowing that a rough night was ahead for all of us, I accepted his offer of some free takeout, went home, got dad settled and fed mom in the car before taking her to the ER. She wasn't likely to get any dinner otherwise. Sure enough, the hip was broken. Crisis. Dad could manage at home for the moment with the help of the paid caregivers. I quickly rearranged my schedule. Of course, I always knew something like this could happen at any moment, but that doesn't mean it's any easier when it actually does.

Caring for an elderly parent, you know in your head that the situation could change on a dime, but that doesn't prevent the onset of that horrible sinking feeling when a crisis actually hits. No one is ever completely prepared for a crisis. Even so, it does help to have systems and plans in place: lists of who to call, extra food in the pantry, suitcase half-packed with the essentials... it all helps. At one point, I even kept extra parking tokens on hand for the local hospital, knowing I'd use them eventually.

If you aren't in crisis at the moment, think ahead about your unique situation. It's very likely that you will be faced with a sudden crisis at some point in your caregiving years, and the more you can do to have plans in place, the better things will be when the time comes. Look at this list, and think about what might help and what you could add to it to best suit your unique situation. It's all about making *your* life easier, so don't stress. Pick and choose what works for you.

- Carry a copy of medical proxy and/or living will documents with you at all times. Keep a current list of your loved one's medications here too. Remember to update it as needed.
- Refill prescriptions (your own and others') regularly, so that you don't run out if you can't get to the pharmacy for a few days. Always keep at least a week's supply on hand.
- Keep your pantry stocked with a few off-the-shelf meals that can be prepared without lots of extra fresh ingredients in case a crisis hits right before your usual shopping day.

- Keep a list of take-out places that deliver to wherever your parent lives. This is especially helpful if they don't live locally to you and you aren't familiar with the area.
- Also, if you aren't local, keep a suitcase half-packed with toiletries, sleepwear, etc., ready to go quickly if needed.
- Don't let your car's tank drop below half full.
- Keep an extra phone charger with you at all times.
- If you have young children, have a plan in place for who can step in on short notice for babysitting. Talk to this person ahead of time about your situation.
- Have a crisis plan for work. What can be postponed? Who could jump in to help for the things that can't be postponed? Who can you enlist as backup? Who could cover your shift? What could you do online or from a distance?
- Plan a family phone tree or group text, so that you, the caregiver only have to tell the detailed story once, not over and over again. A private family/close friends Facebook or other online group is also helpful for passing along news. Make sure that older relatives who aren't tech savvy are informed.
- Keep a granola bar or two in your glove compartment (something not covered with chocolate if you live in a warm climate) or with your emergency documents.
- Stash a little cash there too, some small bills for vending machines and a few dollars in change.

As important as physically preparing for a crisis is, your mental preparation is equally, if not more, important. Oftentimes, a crisis is a hurry-up-and-wait situation, where you rush to the ER, or rush to meet the doctor, surgeon, appointment of some sort, only to find yourself cooling your heels in a waiting room once you're there. Mentally navigating a crisis begins with recognizing this common dynamic and using it to your advantage. Wait time can be a time to actively calm down, catch your breath and engage in a little self-care.

Step out; get a breath of fresh air. Slow your breathing. Count to five on the in-breath, pause, and again on the out-breath. Do it again. Keep it up for a few minutes. Stretch. (A quick online search of "office stretches" will give you ideas of stretches you can do without special equipment and in public.) If you pray, pray. If you meditate, meditate. Even if you aren't the prayer or meditation type, most hospitals offer a non-denominational chapel that can be a quiet refuge in times of crisis.

Your needs matter in a crisis. You can't help your loved one if you are falling apart at the seams. If you are an outgoing extrovert, you will find people willing to talk in waiting rooms. It's amazing how strangers can bond in a time of crisis, and you may find yourself being comforted as you comfort others. Reach out. On the other hand, if you are a more introverted sort, you are under no obligation to talk to anyone if you don't want to. If fending off chatty folks isn't your cup of tea, you can minimize contact by sitting with your back to people if possible, or heading for the chapel or even a small family conference room for some privacy. Closing your eyes also helps. Worst comes to worst, simply say, "Thank you, but I'm not in a talkative mood now."

Most important in a crisis is to realize that you rarely have to make a decision *right now.* Decisions will certainly have to be made, but the vast majority of the time, even in extreme crises, you can take a half hour to simply think things through. Most times, you can take a few hours or even a day or two to decide what the best course of action may be. Take that time. Ask for it. Slow down. Slow down. Slow down. Breathe deeply. You are stronger than you realize.

Questions to consider:

- Do you have a "crisis plan" in place? Does it need an update?
- How can you raise the level of your own self-care in a crisis to match the level of stress you have to endure?
- Who comes to mind as someone you can call in a crisis for some active support for you, the caregiver? Ideally, this is someone a little detached from the situation who can focus on supporting you.

Tags: at the hospital, crisis, planning ahead, self-care, stress

It Is Imperfect

For three years, I made weekly caregiving trips to my parents' home. It began in the aftermath of dad's fall and broken hip, and continued with the diagnosis of mom's dementia, and eventually her first broken hip. They were determined to stay in their home FOREVER. Whenever I would broach the subject of them moving closer to me, or to an assisted living place in their town, dad would counter with, "We have everything we need right here!" Inside my head, I would think, "yeah, including a daughter who's making it possible!"

Over the course of those three years, the situation gradually deteriorated. The whole elaborate arrangement of caregivers, visiting nurses, therapists, clergy, neighbors, family and friends (not to mention me) hung by a thread. When would it snap? It seemed that I was working harder and harder and still things were getting worse and worse.

I consider myself a recovering perfectionist, and one of the key experiences that helped kick me into "recovery" was learning to accept that I couldn't fix everything with my parents. I couldn't make everything right, no matter how hard I tried, and believe me, I tried. Dad didn't like what the caregivers cooked? I would put a dinner in the slow cooker before I left for the week. Next week, I'd try another recipe if he didn't like the one I made. The kitchen floor was dirty? I'd mop it. The clothes were wrinkly from the dryer? I would iron them. Oh wait. They shouldn't be put in the dryer at all. I'll hang them on the line instead, then iron them. The lawn guy did a lousy job again? We'll find someone else. Mom needed her hair done? Add "mom's hairdresser" to the list of appointments to make and keep, right after the eye doctor, the foot doctor, the dentist, the primary care doctor, the outpatient blood tests, the annual VA appointment, the orthopedist, the cardiologist, the car inspection, the caregiver agency and the elder law consult.

It was utterly exhausting, and still things were getting worse. I would arrive to find that mom had clearly not bathed for the entire week I was away, despite repeated instruction to the caregivers, who told me that she simply refused. Stains on the carpet testified to spills and accidents that they tried to clean up without success. The pillbox was still half full and forgotten. The whole place literally stank.

Aside from worries about the precarious situation, it drove my perfectionist self crazy. Here I was, knocking myself out, and if only everyone would just listen and do what I told them the way I told them to do it... but of course, they didn't.

I began a new ritual with a mantra. I would arrive in town, gas the car, then instead of going straight to the house, I'd pull off into the parking lot of a nearby church and just sit for five minutes. I would try to collect myself to face whatever I would face that week. With each breath, I began to repeat to myself a new mantra, "It is imperfect." At first, it was a statement of fact, an acknowledgement of reality. I was coming face to face with all that I could not control and just saying it out loud. After a few months, one day I spontaneously added "...and that's okay" to the phrase.

If we love the people we are caring for, we desperately want to make everything as good as it can be for them. We want to fix it all. We want things to be just right. They, in turn, may want everything to stay exactly as it has always been, or they may not want to bother us and try to fix things themselves, only to make matters worse, and leaving us to pick up the pieces.

It helps to really face what we can and can't control. Simply acknowledging to ourselves, over and over if needed, what our own limits are, can help us to accept them. Try this: make two lists: one of what you can and one of what you cannot control. For example, I can refill prescriptions and make sure they are up to date. I can't control whether she takes her pills when I'm not there. I can make a dentist appointment for dad. I can't control whether or not we will arrive on time (something may happen at the last minute and cause a delay). I can hire someone to clean. I can't control whether or not they'll do a good job.

Seeing what we can and can't control written out on paper helps give us some perspective. The next step is to let go of those things that, in the big picture, are less of a big deal than we thought. The dusting for example, or the wrinkly clothes really are small potatoes, but even if we let go of the small stuff, we still need to mentally release even the bigger things as being out of our control. We may remove the loose rugs from the bathroom, yet mom still falls. We may keep a critical doctor's appointment, but dad still ends up in the ER the next day. We may carefully make sure they take their pills, only to discover they took a double dose when we weren't looking.

So much is out of our control. There is no "perfect" to be found here, no matter how hard we try. Working ourselves into the ground won't change that. The only thing we really have control over is our own response to whatever presents itself. First and foremost, we need to give ourselves permission to be our imperfect, very human selves. We need to give ourselves permission to leave the mess as it is because we're just too tired to face it, or to simplify by not doing things they way we've always done them in the past. You are doing the best you can, and it is enough. All of it is imperfect, every last messy, out of control bit of it, and that really is okay.

Questions to consider:

- What things or situations can you let go of, and simply allow it to be what it is? The answer to this may be as mundane as letting the dust pile up on the knick-knacks, or as serious as saying no to an invasive medical test for your parent.
- Make the two lists described above. How do they compare? Are there things on one side that really belong on the other?
- What mantra can you say to remind yourself that you're doing the best you can? Create one and use it.

Tags: autonomy and control, rituals and traditions, self-care, stress

The Thread Snaps

For a little over three years, since dad first fell and shattered his hip, the situation at the house had been hanging by a thread. Slowly, slowly that thread wore ever thinner as one issue after another added new stresses. Mom was diagnosed with dementia. She too broke a hip. Dad was forced to stop driving. Caregivers were brought in, first twice a week, then daily. I had been making the weekly 100 mile trek for that entire time, handling everything from finances and medical appointments to grocery shopping and laundry, and my own energy was waning.

Any rational observer could see that the situation was incredibly fragile, and becoming more so with each passing day. I knew it too. The only question was when the thread would snap, and how the details would play out.

It finally happened one hot August day, about a week before my teaching semester was due to start. I was out with my younger son, getting his high school senior portraits taken when my cell phone rang. Mom had fallen in the living room. Fortunately, a visiting nurse happened to be there at the time, and had called an ambulance. It would turn out to be another broken hip, the opposite side from the first. That's it, I thought. This being "my" third hip break, I knew very well what was involved in rehab, and I knew the situation needed to change, and fast. Thankfully, I already had some plans in place. We finished the photo shoot. It took about a half hour, and during that time, I roughed out a plan to get through the next few weeks.

If you've been at this caregiving stuff a while, you probably know that at some point, things will break down. The living situation will become unworkable. Maybe your parent is living alone. Maybe he/she is living with you. Whatever it is, you can probably see it coming. It's unusual that a parent goes from completely 100% independent and healthy to totally disabled in one swoop (although it does sometimes happen). More likely is a scenario where things have been on a downhill trajectory in fits and starts for some time, until an event forces the situation to a tipping point.

As sad as this is to witness, the fact that it is somewhat predictable works in your favor. You can see it coming. You know the changes that are likely to happen for your individual situation, and more importantly, you can plan for them. If you don't already have power of attorney, get it now. It will make your life much easier as time passes.

If the living situation needs to change, where would you want your parent to live? Where would they want to live? If they live alone now, would they need to move in with you? What would that look like? Do you need to make any modifications to your home? The time to do it is now, *before* you need it. Imagine walkers and wheelchairs. Are the doors wide enough? Imagine bathrooms, grab bars and bath seats. If your parent has dementia, issues like security and wandering come into play. You may need to add safety locks to the stove, or block off access to entire rooms. Is this a workable situation for you, with the rest of your life? Think long and hard on this before you commit for the long haul.

If they would move to a facility, what would that be? Assisted living? Nursing care? Something semi-independent but still with some support? What can they afford? Where is the best place near you? Or would it be in their hometown? There are a million questions, and they all have answers, but it may take time to find out what they are.

I know that as a caregiver, you are likely crazy-busy, up to your eyeballs in any number of tasks, but the biggest favor you can do for your future self is to think about and investigate things ahead of time. Figure out the finances. What assets do they have? How does Medicare differ from Medicaid? What rehab places are "in-network" for your parent? Would the move be in-town or across country? A move across state lines complicates matters, and you should probably consult a lawyer on both ends to avoid problems like a scenario where your power of attorney is recognized in one state but not the other.

If you are thinking of assisted living or nursing care (and you should be at least thinking about it), what's the best place in your area? Take some tours. Do some research. Learn which places are for-profit and non-profit. I strongly recommend non-profits in general if you can find one. Ask what happens when your parent's finances are drained and they can no longer afford the rent. Could they stay or would they be (politely) shown the door?

If a really good place has a long wait list, consider putting in an application ahead of time. Your parent will slowly work their way to the top of the list, and most likely can stay at the top once they're there. It's not helpful if the best place in town has a 2-year wait list, and you need a placement next week.

It can be utterly overwhelming, but anything you can do ahead of time will lighten the load in the long run. Break the task down into a manageable chunk. Long before the thread snaps, spend a half hour or so every week on research. Knowledge is power and peace of mind. Having some sort of rough plan in your head, and having done a little legwork ahead of time can be a huge stress-reliever for you in the midst of an overwhelming crisis.

If the thread snaps, and you find that you haven't done all the research ahead of time, bear in mind that you don't have to make permanent decisions in the moment. Find a temporary situation that can hold for a few weeks. Most rehab necessary after a major surgery will buy you that kind of time. Use the time to figure out the next step, whatever it may be. Use the resources that you do have, like hospital social workers, who can direct you to other agencies and/or people who can help. Even if you feel alone, you really aren't.

Questions to consider:

- Are you by nature an organized person? A planner? Or does a sibling better fit that description? Think of who in your parent's circle of caregivers is best suited to the research and planning tasks, and delegate if you can.
- Do you think research and planning qualifies as self-care for you? Why or why not?
- What aspects of your individual care situation make your task easier? What make it more difficult? Each situation is unique, and having a realistic grasp of it is key.
- Given your parent's unique medical history, is there anything that you can see coming "from a mile away" in terms of their needs that you can begin to plan for and research?

Tags: at the hospital, crisis, nursing home, planning ahead, systems and structures

The Conversation

The thread had finally snapped. Mom's second hip break would turn out to be THE event that finally forced major changes. I knew it the second I got the phone call telling me what had happened. Dad, on the other hand, took a little more time.

When I arrived at the house, he was visibly shaken. I comforted him as best I could, then hurried up to the hospital. He stayed behind. I realized that the conversation we needed to have would go better if I had some back up. I called his minister, a wonderful woman who would be a great help and comfort to all of us in the days and years to come. She came by later that day, and we gathered in the living room. I asked dad how he thought he and mom would manage. He answered that they would figure it out, make it work somehow, like they had always done before.

"I can't do this anymore," I responded. "I found you an assisted living apartment. We're moving you and mom. I'm sorry, but this is it. I just can't do this anymore." He nodded. He didn't argue at all. In his heart of hearts, he knew that it was time. His minister jumped in, saying all the right things that I couldn't because I was so choked up.

Over the next week, he said his goodbyes. His church threw a party, and gave him a memory book. Lots of people promised to keep in touch. Many of them did. Some would keep in touch by mail or phone; others would come to visit in person. For his part, dad handled it all with grace, never shedding a tear on the day we finally backed out of the driveway of his beloved house, the one he helped to build, for the last time. He would never again see it or his hometown.

Loved ones who are cognitively intact, not suffering from dementia, often know deep down that eventually change will come, even as they fight against it. They may want to postpone it to the last possible moment, to cling to their old life, the life that's comfortable as a favorite sweater, as familiar as a pair of well-worn slippers.

Sometimes a parent responds to a logical argument, but most of the time logic flies out the window and the decision of where and how to live takes on a deeper, more gut-level intensity. You may know that the old homestead just isn't practical anymore. It has too many stairs, or a big yard that needs a lot of work, or a basement laundry room. When you point out these things, you get stony stares in response. So, you muddle until muddling is no longer an option. Whatever event precipitates an unwanted change is likely a very traumatic one for your parent. Resist the urge to say I told you so.

Even if they've moved many times in their lives, the move necessitated by aging is different. This time, they aren't moving to a new job, or to a bigger place because a baby's on the way. This time, the move makes their world a little smaller. If they move in with you or another family member, they may have a loving home, but they are no longer the master of it. They will live surrounded by other people's furniture rather than their own things. If they move to assisted living or a nursing home, they may lose privacy. We as adult children need to be sensitive to these losses, and handle them with as much gentleness as we can muster, and allow them to say goodbye to their old life in a way that suits them.

Saying goodbye for them may involve a farewell party like it did for my dad. Saying goodbye may involve giving them time to pack and sort out what to keep and what to let go, but oftentimes this isn't an option for a parent who needs to go directly from the hospital to their new residence. You can try to soften the blow by taking photos of every room of the old place, and presenting them sometime later on when they have settled in to the new. More immediately, you can try to bring some favorite things along, like a favorite chair and some family photos to decorate the walls.

Don't be surprised if they are angry and miserable with the change at first, no matter how badly needed it was. It may take them time to come to terms with the permanent nature of the move, and it's entirely possible that they never will. It's important to remember that *you* cannot *make* them happy, no matter what you do. Some elders can be miserable no matter where they are (and do their best to make you miserable too). Others can find the silver lining. Ultimately, what they do or do not do in response to a big move is out of your control.

Often, the root of any lingering unhappiness is found deep in the past, far beyond your reach. Regrets for things done and not done, melancholy over the road not taken, sadness for the passing of time:

all these may be influencing your parent on some level, and all of them are beyond your ability to change or impact. Sometimes, it's simply a response to the indignities that come with aging in a society that does not value its elders in any meaningful way.

Probably the most important thing you can do at this point is to "hold space" for your parent. By this I mean to give them the time and space they need, without judgement, to adjust to the needed changes in their own time. This of course is easier said than done. It means resisting the urge to point out how much better everything is now (even if it is a lot better for YOU, the caregiver). It means not getting drawn into arguing. It means providing a strong, supportive container for their emotions, to the extent that you are able, even as you process your own thoughts and feelings about the big change.

Questions to consider:

- How is your experience of a "big move" different from your parent's? If a move hasn't yet happened, how do you imagine the difference might be?
- What has been lost and what has been gained by whatever big changes or moves your parent has experienced?
- How can you help your parent process and grieve the many losses and changes of aging? How are you yourself processing and grieving those same changes?

Tags: anger, autonomy and control, crisis, family dynamics, moving, through their eyes

"I Need a Connection."

The thread had finally snapped. Mom had fallen, again, and broken her other hip. She had the surgery to set the hip, and was ready to be released from the hospital. The BIG MOVE was underway, the one that would finally at long last (from my point of view anyway) get them out of their house and into a safer environment with better care.

The plan was for her to be transported from the hospital by ambulance to a temporary nursing home where she would reside for a week or two, until a bed opened up at the facility that would be her permanent new home. She would spend the journey of 100 miles strapped to a gurney in the back of the ambulance accompanied by an EMT, and I would be there to meet her when she arrived. Admittedly, it wasn't a fantastic option, but it was the best I could manage, and the move had to happen one way or another. She would be well tended, well medicated, and safe.

I spent that day on the phone with the powers-that-be on both ends, working out the details of the transport (in between meeting my own classes and beginning the new fall semester) then going to the temporary facility to sign the standard mountain of paperwork. It was an exceptionally busy day, a pattern that became the new normal as the fall progressed.

Finally, the ambulance arrived. I saw mom come through the door, attended on both sides by young male EMTs: the tattooed, rough around the edges, beefy variety who could lift anyone onto the gurney with ease. She saw me, and her face registered a look of pure and utter relief. She reached out to me.

"Am I glad to see you! Hold my hand. I need a connection."

With that, she grabbed my hand in a vice-grip surprisingly strong for one so frail, and held onto me, eyes closed, as the staff directed us to her room. The burly EMTs plunked her efficiently into her bed, and after a few more papers were signed, I went back in to be with her. Once again, she said, "Hold my hand. Just hold it. I need a connection."

So I did. I sat there, next to her bed, and we held hands for a half hour or so until she fell back asleep, still groggy from the heavy doses of pain medication she was given for the journey. We didn't talk. We just held hands. After a while, my hands got sweaty. It didn't matter.

Connection. That was the word she used. I need a connection. Simple. Basic. A human touch. Looking at the incident from her point of view, the trip must have been bewildering. Foggy from medication, confused by dementia, the moving vehicle, the strange voices, strange faces, strange places all blurred together into a terrifying haze.

Sometimes what our parents need from us isn't complicated. Sometimes what we ourselves need isn't complicated either. It's a connection. It's a hand to hold. When we are exhausted from caregiving, emotionally at the end of our rope, ready to collapse, we can just sit together, lay our hand on theirs and just be. It can be a comfort to both of us, an echo of days gone by when we were the child, and needed a soothing touch to make it all better.

Hold on. Breathe in, breathe out. Keep holding on. Repeat.

One of the best things about simply sitting together quietly, your hand across theirs, is that it is do-able even when we are at our wits end. There are many times in the caregiving journey where we find ourselves just DONE. Tapped out. We are at our wit's end, and yet we are still needed. Somehow, we've got to keep going. Somehow, we've got to find the strength and the will to go on. We've got to reach deep inside and find the strength some way, somehow. We aren't sure how. We don't know the way. It feels like we're reaching so deep inside that we're reaching all the way down to our toes. We are struggling, ready to give up.

Pull up a chair next to the bedside. Make it the best chair you can find. Push it as close as you can. Face to face or looking out together, it doesn't matter. Now sit. Put your hand on hers. Tell her that you're tired. Tell her that you just need a connection, and that you're going to just sit there, quietly together. Tell her that you need her. Breathe in, breathe out. Repeat. The silence itself is restful. Breathe in and out again, slowly. And again. And again.

On some level, maybe overtly, maybe subconsciously depending on the situation, your parent knows how hard you are trying. If your relationship is a good one or even an okay one, then there is a lot of love and sympathy present between you, along with a wish from your parent that your burden wasn't so heavy, and a wish to help in some tangible way. If your relationship was bumpy in the past or still is, there may be other more complicated emotions in the mix: old fears, resentments, complicated passive-aggressive games, and the baggage of generations now writ large in the present. By simply holding hands and establishing a physical connection, you can offer and receive comfort on a deep level, underneath all the emotional noise of the situation. Down deep, at the level of hand-in-hand, connections are renewed. No words are needed. No arguments. No long discussions. Here, we can feel a pulse, a heartbeat. It is enough for now. It is a connection. It gets us through the crisis of the moment, until we can pause for some more extended self-care.

Questions to consider:

- Think back to a time when you were utterly at the end of your rope. What pulled you through?
- Who is your connection?
- What does "comfort" mean to you?

Tags: comfort, crisis, nursing home, self-care

Big Changes

The big move from house to assisted living/nursing home happened in pieces. Mom was discharged directly to a temporary nursing home to await an open bed in the place where she would live permanently. We moved dad into a one-room efficiency apartment in the assisted living section of the large complex where mom would eventually be. A few days later, we moved his furniture. He adjusted amazingly well, and made friends quickly. It didn't hurt that he was one of only a few men in the building, and his arrival prompted a flurry of attention from the female residents, a boost to his ego that helped to smooth the transition considerably. He also bonded with the other men, and shamelessly flirted with the female staff and residents alike. He quickly got himself elected to the "Resident's Council" and set about fixing everything that he deemed in need of his attention.

Mom moved to the nursing section the following week. Dad visited her daily, a ritual that would persist until his own permanent move to nursing care a year later. Every day he would tell her the story of her fall and broken hip, and how he was in the next building but would see her every day. Every day, she was visibly relieved to see him drive up in his motorized wheelchair. Eventually, mom settled in and actually blossomed. With regular meals and activities, she put on weight and most of the time was fairly content with her surroundings, even if she had no idea how she got there or why.

When the BIG move, the one from relative independence toward a higher level of care happens for your parent, it's obviously a huge change for them. It's also a major change for you, the adult child caregiver. This change could coincide with the pivotal role-reversal moment when the parent becomes the child, and the adult child becomes the parent. Or not. That moment may be already in the past, or it may be yet to come. In any case, the first big move *toward* a higher level of care, and *away* from a life of independence is significant. For you, it means looking squarely at the decline of your parent without the possibility of denying it any longer. This person who, for your entire life, has been for the most part vibrant and active, is slipping. You may need to grieve this loss, just as you will grieve other losses yet to come.

Your caregiving will change too. For some the load will lighten once the dust settles. A move to assisted living or nursing care will change your caregiving, but one silver lining of such a situation is that you can focus on being the daughter or son, not the physical caregiver. The staff will handle the day to day tasks of food, bathing, and personal care. If your load isn't getting any lighter on this front, you need to find a better place!

For others, the heavy lifting is just beginning. If the big move was to your house, or alternatively, for you to move back in with your parent (still a move away from independence for them), your life is changing in a major way. You will have to find a way to pace yourself, to conserve your physical, mental and emotional energy, for the road ahead. Remember, there are only 24 hours in a day. You can't get twenty-five, no matter how hard you try. There is a classic book on Alzheimer's disease called *The 36 Hour Day,* but I assure you that it only FEELS like 36 hours. In reality, it's all jammed into 24 challenging hours.

How can you pace yourself? There is no one-size-fits-all sort of answer to this question. What you can do is to look closely at your weekly schedule. What tasks drain you of energy (physical, mental, emotional) and what tasks increase your energy? For one person, their job may be a drain. For another, it may be a source of energy. For some, religious services may be a source of energy. For others, they may be a drain. The important thing is that you find some sort of balance. You cannot (CANNOT) go for any length of time doing only those tasks which drain you. You must make time for something that energizes and relaxes you, that feeds your spirit. This is not an option. I don't want to hear that you are "too busy." You must find this time on a regular (weekly at the very least) basis too, not just a once a month fling.

If you don't, if you insist that you will go full throttle solo caregiving 24-7 for any length of time beyond a week or so, you *will* burn out, and you *will* harm your health, your relationships, your career, and your sanity. Caring full time for your elderly disabled parent is likely one of the most difficult things you will ever do in your life, and to do it well requires finding a way to nourish yourself for the task. Many adult children take on the task of bringing a parent to live with them in their home as a loving duty. Their heart is in the right place, but they wind up exhausted and bitter, and to be honest, an exhausted, bitter caregiver is frankly not the best for your parent either. It's one thing to bring your parent to live with you when they are a healthy, lively 70 year old who can help with babysitting the grandkids. It's something else entirely to bring in a frail 85 year old who needs supervision and 24-7 help.

Whatever form the big move takes, it's a milestone on the caregiving journey. It will take time to adjust to the new normal, to find your legs beneath you, to steady your steps. Give yourself and your parent, some time to make the adjustment. Expect to take at least a month to settle in, possibly longer for a parent with dementia. Don't give up on a living arrangement unless it's been in place at least a month. Give yourself a pat on the back, too. You deserve it.

Questions to consider:

- If you've helped your parent make a big move, has it lightened your load or made it heavier?
- What does "life balance" mean to you? How can you move towards a better balance of where you spend your energy?
- What do you have going on in your life besides caring for your parent? Have those other aspects suffered from your caregiving? Take stock now and then.

Tags: autonomy and control, dementia, moving, nursing home, self-care, stress

Sloppy Grief

Mom was finally settling in. She had gotten used to the routine at the nursing home where she would live for the rest of her life. She saw dad every day, and me three or four times a week. She also saw her grandchildren, her son-in-law, and a parade of family and friends who made the 100 mile trek from her hometown to see her. She would remember none of it. She had a favorite chair in the common living room, and would wave at everyone, friend or stranger, who passed. She went to an exercise class for wheelchair bound residents, and she gleefully devoured ice cream whenever it was offered. She also had absolutely no idea where she was, or how she got there, or why she was there, or what was happening in general. Most of the time, she didn't care.

I was relieved, happy even. For many people, placing their mother in a nursing home would be a cause for sadness, but for me it was a cause for celebration. I knew she was safe. I knew she was well fed, clean and cared for. There was no longer a risk that she would wander off, or burn down the house trying to cook, or let in a stranger who would rob her blind or worse. Never again would I walk into their house and find her smelling a little too ripe from not bathing or changing her clothes for a week.

Over the years since that fateful day when dad first fell, I shed plenty of tears over mom, mostly on the side of the highway headed home. I would pull off the road, put on the flashers and bawl sloppy tears until my eyes ached and my whole head was clogged and then pull myself together again and keep driving. During her nursing home years, I tended to cry a lot in the parking lot. I functioned well enough in the world I suppose, but had little emotional energy as I dragged myself through the days. A few years later, at her funeral, my eyes were dry.

When a loved one has dementia of any type, grief comes early. Alzheimer's disease has been called the long goodbye. It's an appropriate expression. It's a slow, agonizing thing for the caregiver, even when the elder seems to be doing fine. Your experience of dementia as a caregiver will be very different from your parent's experience of dementia.

Some people slip into a sort of happy confusion as dementia slowly takes hold. These are the go-with-the-flow ones, who become almost like Zen masters, living fully in the moment, not worrying about the past or the future. Others drift into the past, reliving significant moments and situations, asking for long-dead relatives and searching for childhood homes. These are the ones who will mistake you, their child, for their own parent if the family resemblance is strong. Still others become a mix of angry and confused, lashing out at anyone and everyone in their never-ending quest for answers that are promptly forgotten. These ones may become paranoid, believing that everyone is keeping secrets from them. Most confusing are those who flip between these various ways of being. One day, they are happy, the next paranoid and violent. For you, the adult child, it's exhausting.

Regardless of the route taken, the ultimate path of dementia is painfully clear. Your parent is drifting away from being the person you knew. Their personality may change so completely that it becomes hard to remember who exactly the "real" mom or dad is, or was, or whatever... The loss happens an inch at a time. They may have good days and bad days, but zooming out, looking at them over a larger time frame (six months or so) the decline is obvious.

In such a scenario, your grief at this sad state of affairs can be erratic and unpredictable, not following anything resembling nice, neat stages. One day you may feel angry, the next depressed. A week later, your parent will say or do something that throws you back into shock all over again. You may feel numb. You may cry randomly. You may be moody. You may not have the energy to face the rest of your life. Friends, co-workers and even family who don't have direct, personal experience with dementia will find it hard to understand. Especially if they have only brief encounters with your parent, or visited on a good day, people can't always accept or comprehend just how tough it can be to watch your parent drift into oblivion an inch at a time. These well-meaning folk will regale you with comments like, "She didn't seem so bad to me. Are you sure she has Alzheimer's?" or "He told me you never visit at all. You really should visit more often." Try not to strangle them on the spot.

What is there to do when you are grieving in a society that doesn't quite believe you have cause for it yet? After all, you still have your parent, right? People will remind you of that. It's true that you have a person who looks like your parent, who wears your parent's face and carries your parent's name, but down deep you know in your heart of hearts that something, some key essence, is missing. That mysterious something that you can't quite describe or name, has already died, and with it, a part of your parent died too. A few months later, you realize that something else, another piece, is also missing, and has died. It's like a thousand piece puzzle from which pieces are being taken away one at a time, until lots of little details of the picture are lost, and eventually whole sections are missing. When does the person die? Is it when the first bit of personality is lost, something you only know in hindsight, or is it when they finally take the last breath? Perhaps it is somewhere in between.

Grieving the loss of a parent to dementia is a sloppy sort of grief. It doesn't fit anyone's timetable or pattern. It is incomplete, a half-grief. It isn't recognized by our culture. It helps to seek support online or in person from others who are dealing with similar situations. Talking to someone who knows, who *really* knows what it's like can be incredibly cathartic. Take whatever support is offered. Be gentle with yourself, and let yourself grieve in whatever way, whatever form you need. Recognize the grief for what it is, the pain over the loss of someone you love. It may be sloppy, but it is absolutely real.

Questions to consider:

- Are you experiencing grief, even though your parent is still living? In what ways?
- Does the face you present to the world match how you are feeling inside?
- How does your experience fit with the experience of your siblings if you have them? Are you all experiencing similar feelings? How do your experiences differ?

Tags: dementia, grief, nursing home

Diplomacy

For the most part, dad was happy. Except when he wasn't. Overall, he had adjusted to assisted living pretty well. He would visit mom every day in nursing care, then go back to his own tiny apartment. He was making new friends, going to activities, and seemed to be relieved not to have to worry about mom's day-to-day care. The only dark clouds in this sunny sky were the new rules: things like mandatory fire drills that woke him up from his naps.

The most frustrating for him were rules about medications. The aides would dutifully show up pills in hand and make sure he took his meds on time, which was actually an improvement from my perspective. For prescription medications, it made sense. The problem was that the rules applied to all medications, prescription and over the counter. Even something as benign as a cough drop was considered a "medication" and required a doctor's approval. This was too much. He could handle his own cough drops, foot lotion and muscle rub all by himself thank you very much. On this, I agreed with him, frankly. It did seem a bit silly from his perspective. From the perspective of the larger institution, though, things looked different. It made sense that the staff know who was taking what, and what meds were kept in everyone's apartments since these were frequently left unlocked. There were some residents with dementia, and what if they wandered in and found something harmful? If they allowed X, what about Y? It was a slippery slope for sure.

After a while, my by-the-book, rules-are-rules dad was asking me to smuggle in his favorite forbidden items. This was completely out of character for him, but it reflected his sense that he was not being treated like the adult that he was. I decided to have a delicate talk with the staff. After some negotiations and doctor's approval, he was allowed unfettered access in his apartment to some of his OTC favorites. Needless to say, I was relieved.

Once your parent moves to a nursing home or assisted living, the rules change. Your role as caregiver also changes. The good part is that in general, your load is lighter. The challenge is that your role becomes more complicated. You, the caregiver, are now often in the position of being stuck between institutional bureaucracy and the demands and wishes of your parent.

Most of the rules you will encounter make sense from the perspective of the institution. For example, as an institutional rule, your parent might need two staff members to assist with a transfer from bed to wheelchair. That makes sense from the perspective of the institution wanting to avoid worker's compensation claims from aides injuring their backs lifting heavy residents. Of course, if your mom weighs 90 pounds soaking wet, and she's been in the wheelchair all day and just wants to be put to bed, it makes no sense. But, rules are rules. The low-ranking aides are not going to risk their jobs even if you throw a fit about how ridiculous it is, and throwing a fit only makes things worse.

Situations like this put you in a delicate position. On the one hand, your mom or dad is priority #1 for you, and you want them to receive the best care possible, and for their wishes and wants to be accommodated. On the other hand, if you raise a fuss over every little detail and constantly make their job more difficult, you will earn the label of "problem child" with the staff. Once you earn that dubious honor, you run the risk of being in the position of the boy who cried wolf, only to be ignored when a real wolf appeared.

In general, you want the staff to like you and your parent. If they do, things will go more smoothly, and when you do have an issue, it will be resolved more easily. This doesn't mean that you need to grovel and kowtow, but it does mean that you need to develop some diplomacy skills, and to show as much kindness to the staff as you possibly can, especially the lower level staff who do most of the (literal and figurative) heavy lifting of personal care. Monetary gifts are generally not allowed (no tipping at the holidays), but the occasional plate of cookies for the break room is usually welcome.

If your parent is notoriously stubborn or difficult, you may find yourself feeling like a double agent. You can openly express your sympathy and acknowledge that dad (or mom) can be a royal pain in the... In fact, it would probably be a good thing if you did show the staff openly that you get how hard their job can be. Doing this makes you an ally, with the ultimate goal being better care for your parent. With mom (or dad), show some sympathy there too. Your parent's world is shrinking. They don't have the freedom or physical strength they used to, and this is a legitimate cause for frustration. Lashing out at the staff (and you) is understandable, even if it is difficult to handle.

The ultimate task for you, the adult child caregiver, is to discern when you need to really speak up, intervene and make a stink. You need to pick your battles carefully. When should you take a complaint all the way to the top, loudly? * To help you sort it all out, consider the following and how they apply to your individual issue:

- Is the issue temporary, one that will resolve itself?
- Is the issue one of preference?
- Can you resolve it yourself without violating any institutional policy?
- Does the issue involve safety?
- Is it a comfort issue?
- If you did take it "to the top" and it was resolved, would the resolution make a substantial and ongoing positive difference in your parent's quality of life?
- Can you find a "third way" to help address the real underlying concern?
- What is your parent's temperament, and how does that factor in?
- Consider your own temperament and need for sanity in your own life too.

There are no right or wrong answers. What works for one person may not work for another. Some things are easily solved. For example, if mom doesn't like the tea served in the dining room, maybe you can buy the brand she likes and have her bring that. Others may be intractable, like a parent who absolutely refuses to comply with rules about when/where smoking is allowed. Realize too that there are situations where it is simply impossible to keep everyone happy. Do the best you can and don't beat yourself up about what is beyond your ability to fix.

*Note: the thoughts expressed here are meant to apply to ordinary situations, NOT situations where abuse and/or neglect may be evident. In situations of abuse/neglect, seek medical and legal counsel as quickly as possible. Abuse and neglect are beyond the scope of this book. Nothing said here is intended as medical or legal advice.

Questions to consider:

- How do issues of personal autonomy look from your perspective and your parent's? Are there any similarities? Differences?
- Do you tend to be a rebel and a rule-breaker, or a well-behaved teacher's pet? How about your parent? What impact do personality traits have on situations involving autonomy and control?
- If you have encountered the world of nursing care and assisted living, even on a short term basis, what did you think of the rules? Did they make sense to you?

Tags: autonomy and control, comfort, nursing home, systems and structures, through their eyes

The Stuff of Life

I pulled the car into the garage and shut the door behind me. I didn't particularly feel like talking to the neighbors. I'd already given them an update, and wasn't in the mood to waste time repeating myself or offering new details just to provide grist for the gossip mill. The BIG move was behind us. Mom was settled into the nursing home; dad was making new friends in assisted living. Now, all I had to do was to deal with the house. Clear it out, clean it up, sell it. No big deal. Piece of cake. Ha!

The place was in total disarray. The move had come on the heels of an emergency (mom's second broken hip) and was sort of a grab-it-and-go project where anything non-essential was simply abandoned. There was nothing orderly or organized about it at all. There was still dirty laundry in the baskets, food in the fridge, and dying flowers in the patio containers. Mail was piling up. The closets were still full of clothes. We had only packed up a suitcase-full. Mom didn't really need much. Dad needed far less than before.

I stood there in the living room for several minutes, not knowing what to do first. My gaze eventually landed on a glass sitting next to where dad's chair used to be. It had about an inch of water in it, the leftovers of melted ice. I picked it up, and took it to the kitchen. I found dirty dishes in the sink. Okay, that's it. I'll do the dishes. It's a start.

At some point in your caregiving years, you may be tasked with cleaning out the family home, alone or with others. This may happen after a death, or long before, as it did for me. If it was your childhood home, the task may have many emotional layers to it; you might find yourself feeling like an archaeologist, digging deeper and finding more all the time.

It can be tempting to call in the professionals. There are plenty of people who will completely clear out and clean up a house for a price, leaving you with a realtor-ready place. This choice may be the right one for you if distance, time constraints or sibling conflicts makes the task just too much to bear. However, if you choose this option, you are missing out on a chance for a unique experience, one that can bring healing and growth if you let it.

I don't want to sugar-coat it. Taking this on involves lots of plain old grunt work: scrubbing icky crud, hauling loads to whatever charity accepts boxes of random yet still useful stuff, moving heavy objects... Don't kid yourself. It isn't all epiphanies and enlightenment, but epiphanies do come unbidden and enlightenment creeps into an open heart.

Clearing a house after a big move or a death is a process, not something accomplished in an hour or a day, so pace yourself. There's lots of work to be done, and not all the work is physical. The objects you sort may have emotional resonance beyond any physical value. You may encounter items you haven't seen in decades, or objects from your childhood. If you run across something that suddenly strikes a deep emotional chord, hold it for a while in your hands, then set it aside for now. You can throw it out later. Give yourself a chance to be with it for just a little while. Let memories surface. Allow yourself to be nostalgic. The process of sorting and clearing can help you process the emotions of the change you and/or your parent have just experienced. It is emotional work, I daresay spiritual work, to clean out a loved one's home. It should be acknowledged and honored as such.

Clearing a house is also a chance to get to know the former resident (aka your parent) in a deeper way. You may be surprised at what you find, and the insights that come with it. You may discover old family records, photos or memorabilia that you didn't know existed. Even something as dull as an old checkbook can give a glimpse into the past. What you find may help you see your parent in a new light, and get a sense of your family history in an up-close and personal way. Even as adults, it can be hard to see our parents simply as fellow humans. Sorting and clearing stuff can help with that process.

Unfortunately, what you find may not all be pleasant. You may find evidence of infidelity, or a stash of alcohol that confirms your long-held suspicions. You may find that your parent is not the person you thought they were. It may not be easy, but seeing your parent clearly may help you sort out your feelings about the past. Discovering that dear old dad had a serious drinking problem may help explain why he acted the way he did when back when you were a kid. The truth may not be easy, but it really can be liberating to know it. Our parents are human after all, with flaws and faults. They made mistakes. They had regrets. They had issues and struggles of their own. Knowing this helps you to see them clearly. What you do with that understanding is up to you. It isn't something you have to fully comprehend and process at the time of clearing the house. It's a task that may take many years, and that's okay.

You may also run across items that, for various reasons, you simply destroy without looking more closely at them. For example, you may discover a box of love letters, and feel that you don't want to invade your parent's privacy by reading them. Or you may come across financial records from that one uncle who had some shady business dealings, and decide that it's just better not to go there at all, and toss them into the trash. These are completely valid choices, and by making them, you express your own values and preferences. You are in charge here. There is no right or wrong, only what you decide.

In the end, it's the process that matters, the experience. Take it a step at a time, a room at a time, a drawer at a time, and in the middle of it all, pause and reflect on the story told by all the stuff. It's the story of a life, your parent's life. On some level, it's your story too.

Questions to consider:

- Do you find it easy or hard to let go of physical stuff like memorabilia? Why do you think you are the way you are?
- If you have siblings, have you discussed with them how to go about sorting out the family treasures? Are you in agreement about the approach? If not, can you strike a compromise?
- If you cleaned out your parent's home, what item(s) gave you insight into your parents as people? What did you learn?
- Did you have any big insights after doing a clean/clear out? Anything that will stick with you?

Tags: autonomy and control, family dynamics, mindfulness, moving

The Tale of the Table

I confess. I did it. I ate takeout off of the bare-naked dining room table, and I have no regrets.

The table was made of pecan wood, purchased in the seventies, probably on an easy payment plan or maybe layaway. It wasn't cheap. It was solid. Sturdy. And for my parents, very expensive. The table sat six, eight, or even ten if we really squished in close when cousins came to visit. Decades worth of Thanksgiving turkeys with homemade gravy had graced it, along with Christmas pies, moved-indoor-because-it-rained picnics, birthday cakes and the occasional obligatory post-funeral brunch. Through it all, the table was a presence in my childhood.

Except that I never actually saw it. The table, that is. It was hidden underneath the thick protective cover. A spill at the table caused my mother to spring into action. Quick!! Grab the towels! Sop up the mess! Save the tabletop! And diligently, with great apology from the spiller, we would run for towels and gingerly lift the pad, peeking at the precious wood. Did the spill soak through? No? Whew.

Over the years, the cover (which was never particularly attractive in the first place) got shabbier and shabbier. In recent years, it was held together with tape. Ugly. Ugly. Ugly. Underneath it, the tabletop was safely protected, and that was what mattered.

Now, I was tasked with emptying the house and getting rid of the table along with everything else left behind after the big move. I sorted. I boxed. I hauled loads to the curb. I held an auction. The auctioneer carefully briefed me on what to expect ahead of time. "Don't be offended at the low offers," he said, "people come to these things looking for a bargain."

Okay, fine. On auction day, I hid in the bedroom with the door closed, because it was just too emotionally exhausting to watch at first. After a while, I decided to peek. Yes, things were sold for a song, but I was prepared and it didn't bother me. I was not offended by the low offers.

Then, the auctioneer and his small herd of buyers made their way to the dining room, where the pristine tabletop was seeing the light of day for the first time in decades. Any bids for the table and six chairs? $200? (What a deal!) No? $150? (c'mon people!), No? $100? (Are you serious?) $50? $25? Awkward silence... "I'll give you $5 and haul it off," said a young male voice. Okay, now I am offended.

This particular low offer was just too much for me to stomach. I stepped in and turned him down before the auctioneer could accept the offer. I'd rather donate it than sell it so cheaply. The herd moved on to the next room, and I just stood there staring at the glorious, shiny table, looking brand new. A wave of sadness swept over me.

All those dinners. All those spills. All those frantic runs to the kitchen for towels to sop up the gravy. All the turkeys and pies and birthday cakes. All the schoolbooks and mail. All the life. And here it was, that gorgeous tabletop, protected from it all, looking smooth and polished and so shiny I could see my face reflected in it.

The following week, my husband joined me for a day of sorting and packing the auction leftovers, and we did it. We ate a meal of takeout sushi right off the bare-naked, shiny, perfect, not a scratch on it, downright virginal tabletop. I think we even spilled a little soy sauce.

My mother was, like many of her generation, self-deprecating and frugal. There were many things of hers that were "too nice" to use. So she didn't. Fancy gift soaps would accumulate dust in decorative bowls in her bathroom until they lost their scent. Padded hangers hung empty in the back of her closet behind the wire ones tangled with clothes. And of course, there was the table, that shiny gorgeous table. Too nice to use.

I've spent many hours ruminating over the table and its meaning. Frugality explains part of the story, but not all. The table was a chunk of wood. A thing. An object. Why did it exist? What was it for? The table forced me to consider my relationship with all the stuff in my life.

We all have stuff in our lives: stuff that we use (the utilitarian stuff), stuff that we treasure (the precious stuff) and stuff that we sort of hang onto out of a sense of social obligation, family duty or guilt (the obligatory stuff).

For me, the table embodied the intersection of all three of these categories. It was utilitarian. After all, we ate from it, even if it was covered up. It was precious, the repository of memories. But it was also obligatory. We were duty-bound to protect it, and felt guilty when we spilled the gravy. How different would it have been if we could have let go of that mindset, tossed away the ugly cover, and just enjoyed it as both utilitarian and precious?

How much stuff do we have in our lives that is there because it is either mostly or entirely obligatory? We keep the tea-set from Great Aunt So-and-so because she gave it to us. Never mind that we barely knew her, and that we don't drink tea. My mother never used the fancy gift soaps or the padded hangers because they had somehow slipped from being utilitarian to being obligatory, sort of like the tabletop itself.

At some point in your caregiving journey, you may find yourself sorting out piles and piles of stuff as you empty your loved one's house of a lifetime's accumulation. What to keep? What to donate? What to sell? What is precious? What is not? Are there objects like my mom's table that fall into more than one category? Are there objects that, over the years, slipped more and more into the obligatory group?

As you sort, some things will be tossed away easily. The old vacuum cleaner that never worked very well will likely end up in the trash without much drama. Ditto for the ugly couch. But what about the jewelry, the book collection, or the old yearbooks?

The silver spoons, the good china or the collectibles?

Ask yourself in what category or categories that these sorts of items belong. Remember that there may be overlap among several categories. Will you use them (really)? Utilitarian. Does the thought of selling them make you intensely sad? Precious. Are they something you *should* keep? Were they really important to somebody else but not to you? Any guilt feelings? Yes? You're into obligatory stuff. Now what?

Consider your relationship to the stuff. Why do you feel the way you do? What are the roots of the sense of obligation? What would you do with it, anyway? If the object at hand falls mostly into the obligatory group, imagine just getting rid of it. Do you feel a sense of relief? Release? Lightness? Then let it go. Acknowledge (maybe even out loud) its former role and its importance to the family, but then let it go on its merry way to the next owner, or even to the trash. Blessings on it, then good riddance. If it helps, take a photo to remember it by.

Later on, when the big job of clearing your loved ones house is over, you may find yourself looking on your own stuff with an equally critical eye. Is it time to lighten the load there too? If you don't use it or love it, maybe it's time to let it go.

Questions to consider:

- What is your own relationship with stuff? Are you a packrat or a tosser?
- Are there any other categories of stuff you would add to the three above?
- How has our postmodern, digital age changed how we as a society think about stuff?

Tags: moving, self-care, stress

Finishing the Pepper

My parents were children of the Great Depression. They were taught frugality of necessity, and they carried that lesson with them their whole lives. They re-used everything: aluminum foil, bits of string, odd buttons, margarine tubs, and scraps of paper. Any useful things, especially food, were simply not wasted. That helps explain how I came to be in possession of the big tin of ground black pepper.

I was cleaning out the kitchen after mom and dad made the big move. Pots and pans would go to my kids for their first apartments. Mismatched odd dishes would go to the second-hand store to find another life. The hand-painted plates that decorated mom's kitchen would now grace my own.

Eventually, I found myself sorting through the spice drawer. True to form, mom had never thrown anything out. Decades old tins of nutmeg, cloves and other rarely used seasonings had worked their way to the back of the drawer. Mom hadn't done much cooking for a while now, so pretty much everything in that drawer was stale, even if it wasn't decades old, with one exception. I found the large tin of cheap store-brand ground pepper, bought by me on a recent shopping trip. It was store brand because... well, frugality. It was large because dad used a lot of pepper at the table (when you're not supposed to eat salt, but you just have to shake lots of SOMETHING on your food) and it was something I knew would be consumed quickly at their house. But now, there it was, newly opened, barely used. The rest of the drawer contents I tossed into the trash without a smidgen of guilt, but the pepper? I just couldn't do it.

It appeared that I had soaked up a bit of their frugality myself. I took the pepper home, and over the course of the next three years, used it up. Whenever I pulled it off the shelf, memories of them and their house, my childhood home, drifted through my mind. When I finally emptied the tin and used the last of the (by now) stale pepper, it felt significant somehow, like a thread of connection to the past had been cut. As I put the tin into the recycle box, I let go a little bit more, and felt a tiny bittersweet pang of nostalgia mixed with grief.

Over the course of those years, using up the pepper became a ritual. It was a simple way to engage with my memories and process my feelings about the changes that were happening in my parents' lives and my own. We need rituals in our lives, whether it is something as elaborate as a high mass in a soaring cathedral or as simple as a cup of tea in the evening.

Rituals are metaphors, symbols of something greater than themselves that serve a function in our lives. For Catholics, the mass represents nothing less than the actual presence of God. The cup of tea may represent comfort, relaxation, or leaving the stress of the workday behind. Rituals can connect us with the past, or help us let go of it. They can help us process difficult changes, and help us cope with the struggles at hand.

Many rituals have the potential to be very healing, but some can also be a negative force. Having a cigarette to relax after a stressful meeting might be a ritual, but it's not a healthy one. If you despise baking, making apple pie from scratch every Thanksgiving out of obligation is a ritual that can lead to resentment rather than happy family times. Oftentimes we get stuck in family rituals and traditions that become hollow shells of their former selves over time. They have outlived their vitality and purpose, but we may still cling to them mindlessly.

Using up the pepper became a ritual, but one with a natural end. Once the pepper was gone, it was over. That was probably a good thing. It served its purpose, and eventually it was time to let it go.

At inflection points in our lives, such as a major change like moving parents out of the family home, or after a death, it's a good time to reflect consciously on the rituals and traditions that were important in the past. What do they symbolize for us? Which do we want to keep unchanged? Which can we adapt? Which do we need to let go?

We need rituals in our lives, but the best ones are ones that are engaged mindfully. Rituals are not simply habits. They are conscious choices, best done with intention and thoughtfulness. Doing something a certain way just because that's the way we've always done it leaves us disconnected and unhappy in the end. Rituals can be consciously created for the purpose of helping us cope with the challenges of caregiving. When I was in the stage of my caregiving years when I was traveling back and forth from my parents' house, I treated myself to a vanilla latte on the way home every week. As I headed north on the highway, every sip was a ritual of self-care. When my years of commuting came to an end, naturally so did the ritual, but it had served its purpose.

Consider your situation. First, look back at the rituals related to your beloved elders and how they lived their lives that you may have adopted unconsciously. Do you always do things the way they did? Take the time to look carefully not only at big holiday traditions, but also little things, like buying a certain brand of coffee or always mowing the yard a certain way. Do these unconscious rituals serve you in your life now? If they do, by all means keep doing them, but if they don't, maybe make a change.

Next, think of creating new rituals that help you in your life right now. Do you need to de-stress? Handle heavy emotional issues? Process grief? Bear up over the long haul? What could be a ritual for you to help with those needs? What could it symbolize? It could be a small reward that you give yourself, like my weekly latte. It could be a project that has a natural end, something like spending a half hour each week sorting old family photos while sipping a glass of wine. Eventually the photos will be sorted and the time will come to an end. It could be a regular journaling practice, or slipping into a house of worship or other sacred space near your workplace over your lunch hour for some peace and quiet. Whatever you do, realize that the ritual exists to serve you and your needs. If at any point in the future it becomes a burden rather than a source of sustenance, it's time to let it go and create something new that serves you better as time passes and life changes.

Questions to consider:

- Do the rituals in your life serve you, or do you serve them?
- How's your self-care right now, in whatever stage of caregiving you are? Could adding a simple ritual or some sort help your stress level?
- How can a good habit become a mindful ritual?

Tags: comfort, healing after loss, mindfulness, rituals and traditions, self-care

Digging the Roses

The house was cleared out and empty. It was almost ready to sell. It had taken me two months of weekend trips to do the job, sometimes alone, sometimes with family help. It was late fall, and I had one more job to do: dig the roses.

In the backyard was a rosebush. The rose was a climber, a pale pink oldie that had overgrown its trellis. It had gnarly roots and serious thorns. It was originally my grandfather's; transplanted (or maybe divided) from his house sometime in the 1970s, and I wanted it for my own garden.

Moving this beast was a job that took several hours. First, we needed to prune off all the many twisted branches, cut them down small and bag them with the other yard waste. Then, we needed to dig out the massive root ball, wrap it and load it into the car.

At the other end, we hauled it out again with great effort, plunked it down into a pre-dug hole, with some fertilizer already mixed in and watered it well, mulched it and hoped for the best. In the process of the move, several large roots were severed. The next spring, it put out a few feeble shoots but not much more. No flowers. Barely any leaves. Three more spring times would pass before the sturdy old rose finally rooted enough into its new soil to really grow. I am happy to report that it is alive and well and blooming beautifully as I sit and write today.

The rosebush to me can represent many things. It can represent all the stuff worth holding onto from all the memories and memorabilia of the past, as well as the stuff to let go. It can also be a symbol of personal transformation, growth and change.

In the course of your sorting, you will find many things, tangible and intangible, from your family that should simply be tossed. Into this category goes the accumulated physical junk of the decades, probably most of what you will encounter in the course of the sorting and clearing. Let it go, let it go, let it go...

You may also unearth painful memories, everything from decades old sibling insults and hurtful words to more serious memories of old pain, teenage depression, anxiety, or even childhood abuse and neglect. If these are still overwhelming or seriously affecting your life right now, seek counseling. It is beyond the scope of this book to offer any medical or psychiatric advice. If, on the other hand, the pain now simply aches like an old scar when you are confronted with physical reminders of the past, then maybe the roses can help.

Think of the old rosebush. The core root ball can represent the core, the good stuff that's worth holding onto. You could think of it as yourself, your deep self, your true center. It is sturdy and strong, despite its gnarly appearance. It has weathered many storms, and will weather many more. The soil in which it was growing represents old ways of facing life that are outgrown, maybe old ways that you learned in your younger years, from the parents you are caring for right now. The soil could represent unhealthy coping mechanisms, a negative outlook, a lack of confidence, or your inner critic. The tangled, twisted branches represent the results in your life right now that result from pulling energy from the old soil. They may represent a lack of confidence, an unhealthy relationship, a bad pattern from the past that persists into today. Whatever they represent for you, they've got to go.

Think of transplanting your core self, your deep self, your true self, out of the unhealthy patterns of the past. First, you've got to cut loose all the tangled branches. These cannot make the transition. They've got to go. They may look pretty on the surface, but they won't help you transplant your true self into a healthier pattern. They'll just suck energy, and make it harder for you to sink deep roots into new soil. Cut them off. Bag them up. Send them off to the compost pile.

Next comes the harder task of extracting yourself from the old soil, the old ways, the old hurts. This is hard work, this digging. You'll sweat and strain. You may wonder if it's even possible. You will have to sever a root or two that can't be pulled out any other way. You will struggle to extract yourself, but it is the work necessary for your soul to thrive, and it takes time.

Once you're metaphorically dug out, then what? What is the new soil? The new garden? What does it represent? Healthier ways of coping, a commitment to self-care, nourishment for body and soul, maybe even ongoing therapy or counseling to provide the life-giving water. It represents a fresh start and a new outlook.

It's important to note that our metaphorical roses, along with the literal ones, take time to settle into the new garden. Growth happens first underground, in our own minds and hearts, in places not always visible to the casual glance. New roots need to grow, to sink their tendrils deep into the soft ground, to learn the new ways. They need water and ongoing nourishment. They need to be well-mulched, protected from the cold. They need patience and care.

The first pale shoots of spring are tender things, cautiously growing. It's the same with new patterns, new ways of being. Be gentle with yourself. Nourish and protect the new growth. In time, you will bloom.

The process of caregiving, whether dealing with your parent directly in person, or indirectly by sorting and clearing a house, provides a unique time in your own life for personal growth and healing. Caregiving affects you, the caregiver, not just your parent. The journey itself offers a unique chance to look deeply into family dynamics, old patterns of being, and the lessons learned (consciously or not) in your family of origin. It provides the possibility of real change and new growth, just like for the roses.

Questions to consider:

- Your family legacy isn't just old dishes and jewelry. It's habits, thought patterns, ways of looking at the world. What is the emotional legacy that your parents have passed on to you?
- Look carefully at the older generation of your family, and the generation before them. Can you see the deep roots of some of your emotional legacy, and why your family is the way it is?
- What aspects of your family's emotional legacy are worth keeping and nurturing, and what do you need to let go?

Tags: encouragement, family dynamics, healing after loss, moving

Releasing the Past

It was time to let go. After listing it for six months during the worst housing market in decades, the house had finally sold. I breathed a sigh of relief. I did one last trip to the house before the closing to check that everything was in order, but also to say goodbye.

Dad had moved the previous fall, and after that he never asked to go back to his home of over 50 years, the house he helped to build himself. It must have been difficult and painful for him, and I trust that he said his goodbyes in his own way. Now it was my turn.

The house had been my only home growing up. It was the house where I was brought from the hospital as a baby, the house where I did my homework and played with my dolls as a child, and the house where I dressed for my wedding. It held countless memories.

It didn't feel right to just lock the door and walk away without somehow noting that this was indeed a major passage not only for my parents, but for me. I decided to say goodbye to each and every room. One by one, I walked into them, paused and called up a memory of that particular space, then said my goodbye aloud. It took time, about a half hour to go through all the rooms even in a small house, but at the end, when I stepped outside and said goodbye to the whole place as I locked the door, I knew I was ready to walk away and move on. The following week I went to the closing, signed the papers and handed over the keys, and that was that.

If you are tasked with selling a family home, especially one that was your childhood home, you may be flooded with emotion throughout the process. Selling any house is a big deal. It's the largest financial transaction most people will undertake in their lives. To do it well requires a certain level of detachment. You need to be calm, cool and professional when it comes to things like inspections, repairs, appraisals, commissions, and the like. You can't get bogged down with emotion when dealing with bankers and realtors, but the emotion is there anyway, just below the surface.

Even if you are clearing out a place that was not your childhood home you may still find yourself struck with the emotion of the task. Something as mundane as a move from a rented apartment may feel significant, if it marks a transition away from independence for your parent.

Simple rituals like the one I did when I walked from room to room can help you, the adult child, process what you are feeling in the midst of a big move. It doesn't have to be a big deal, complicated or religious (although it can be if you choose). It could be something done with friends, your siblings, or even possibly your parent, but it doesn't *have* to involve anyone but you.

What matters most is that you mark the occasion as significant, and acknowledge it as a milestone on your own life's journey. Pausing and noting the significance of a change, without getting stuck in it, is the hallmark of a mindful life.

The changes involved with a big move, especially from a longtime family home, center around letting go. We need to let go of the past in order to fully be present in the present. The past, and the place associated with it, may be filled with pleasant memories or unpleasant ones. Most likely it's a mixture of both.

Our letting go needs to encompass both the good and the bad. It's not healthy to be so stuck in happy nostalgia that we are blind to the joys of the present. It's also not healthy to be a prisoner of painful and unhappy memories so that we cannot move on with our lives in the here and now.

Here are a few ideas to create a personal ritual of letting go. Let them spark your own creativity, and use them as a springboard to create something that is uniquely you.

- With friends, gather to share memories in the place. Afterwards, have a final meal together.
- Use candles, either alone or with others. Light a candle to represent a memory. Blow them out to represent letting go.
- If you have unpleasant memories, write them down on a piece of paper, then burn it in place. If burning is impossible, tear the paper into lots of tiny pieces and flush the pieces down the toilet.
- Walk from room to room as I did. Speak your thoughts aloud, or simply think them to yourself. Say goodbye to each room aloud or silently.

- Offer a verbal blessing in each room to the people who will live there in the future.
- Leave a small housewarming gift for them too. Maybe write a short note wishing them happiness in their new home.
- Sleep over one last time. Bring old photo albums, and spend the evening perusing them.

You get the idea. The point is that you honor the good memories, let go of the bad ones, and move on, fully and completely into whatever comes next. Getting stuck in the past won't serve you in the present.

It's also useful to talk to your parent about whatever they may be feeling about the move. Listen without judgment. They may be frustrated or angry at having to move, or resentful of you for forcing the issue, regardless of how necessary it was. Let them say goodbye in their own way, which may be very different from your way. Giving them their own space is easier if you tend to your own emotional needs. When you have acknowledged and honored the change, you can remain grounded even when your parent is struggling to cope with unavoidable, but difficult changes.

Questions to consider:

- Are there any particular aspects of the past that feel more "stuck" than others to you? How can you let them go?
- How can you hold onto good memories while still moving forward in your own life?
- Do your siblings' memories differ from your own in any significant way? There is no right or wrong here. How can you honor and respect each other's memories?

Tags: family dynamics, mindfulness, moving, rituals and traditions, self-care

The Ice Cream Project

The first summer that mom was in the nursing home and dad was in assisted living was quieter than the previous year. I had emptied the house and sold it, and I was no longer making frantic caregiving trips every week. Both had settled in and adjusted to their new surroundings and were medically stable for the moment. I was finally catching my breath.

Most of my visits up until then had been done with efficiency and time management in mind. Life was busy! I would visit them together three times a week. I came in the afternoons during the time when dad would be visiting with mom, and the three of us would spend an hour or so together. Dad, being dad, tended to dominate the conversation with questions about my work, my kids, and my husband followed by a detailed update on the latest meeting of the Resident Council to which he had been elected. I was also in the habit of joining dad for lunch once a week. Dad was well tended, but I felt a little pang when I thought about mom.

Since things had finally calmed down, I decided to spend some time with mom alone. After careful discussion, we decided to take on a summer project together. Once a week, in the evening after dad had gone, I would come over and bring a sundae from the local soft-serve place. They had 14 flavors of sundaes, and we would try them all, one at a time. The project took the entire summer, but in the end we did it, finally reaching the important conclusion that there really are no bad flavors, even though mom thought that black cherry was particularly good. Dementia took many things from my mother, but her sweet tooth remained intact. Our project was clandestine since dad wasn't allowed to eat sugary treats.

Because of her dementia, it was always a surprise for her every time I would walk in, sundaes in hand, but my brief explanation inevitably got her back on track and she repeatedly agreed that this project was indeed a very worthwhile thing to do. There wasn't a whole lot of talking during these visits. We ate our sundaes, then just sat together for a while. It was a good summer.

Somewhere in the middle of your caregiving journey, you may get a little respite, some time between crises when things are stable and you can breathe. If you're lucky, you may even get several of these blessed periods of calm. What then? What do you do?

At this point, it's important to step back, pause and do a little self-evaluation. Caring for an elderly parent is more often a marathon than a sprint, and you need to tend to your own physical and emotional energy so that you are able to face whatever situation may come up. An exhausted and burnt-out caregiver is really no help to anyone. This is still true when your parent is in nursing care, and professionals do the physical day-to-day caregiving.

How often do you visit? How long are those visits? What do you do when you are there? It can be emotionally draining to spend time visiting your parent in a nursing home. Of course, you need to visit often enough (and randomly enough) to make sure your parent is getting adequate care. In my opinion, for a high quality facility, a weekly visit at unpredictable times to check on your parent is enough to meet that goal. When you drop by, is your parent clean? Fresh? Hungry or thirsty? How does their room look? Check in with different members of the staff. Introduce yourself. Ask a few questions. Stay on top of things, but let them do their job and don't get in the way. If, because of distance, your parent has no one checking in on them regularly, consider making a change. Every nursing home resident needs someone, friend or family, to keep an eye on things even in the best facilities. If you can't be there personally, someone else should.

How often and how long you visit depends on a few factors: your parent's physical and cognitive condition, the state of your relationship, the quality of those visits, and your own emotional limits and needs.

If your parent is cognitively intact but physically disabled, they'll notice how often you visit, and may look forward to those visits as the bright spot of their day or week. On the other hand, a parent who suffers from dementia may not be as aware of your comings and goings. The length of your visits is relevant here too. A visit can be emotionally uplifting but physically draining for a frail elder. The trick is to find the sweet spot between a too-short visit that feels rushed and a long, dragged-out visit that depletes your parent physically. This is especially true for visits with multiple family members, children, pets, etc... A half hour with a four year old can be as draining as two hours with a few adults, even if all your parent does is sit in a wheelchair.

How is your relationship with your parent? Loving? Hostile? Antagonistic? Awkward? Warm? If your relationship with your parent has always been strained and difficult for whatever reason, it's unlikely to change at this point. The person your parent is at age 75, 80, or 85 is probably the same person they've always been. It's unlikely that they will suddenly transform into the parent you've always wanted at this late stage. If you are caring for a parent with whom you have longstanding issues or conflicts, it's okay to keep your visits short and sweet. Really.

What do you do when you visit? It can be awfully hard to keep a conversation going once you've exhausted the usual pleasantries and the family updates. Reminiscing is one option. You could bring an album of old photos, or some old music to share. You might watch a game show on TV together, or maybe a vintage movie. Food also helps. Sharing a treat or a meal can help the visit go smoothly. It's also okay to just sit together and watch the world go by out the window. Be in the moment together. Just be.

Finally, what about you? Are you close to your breaking point? If you are emotionally or physically exhausted from caregiving, it's okay to factor that in when thinking about how often and how long to visit. Maybe even take a break for a week or so just to recharge your own batteries, or limit your visits to an easy activity like watching a favorite TV show together. Your needs matter too. You aren't doing your parent any favors if every visit is tense, awkward and draining.

There is no one right way to do this task of caregiving. The trick is figuring out what works for you, your parent, and your individual situation.

Questions to consider:

- What is your experience of visiting your parent? Is it enjoyable or draining (or both)? How can you balance your needs with your parent's needs?
- Consider your parent as a potential resource for family history. Even a parent with dementia can often recall long-ago memories without trouble. Is there anything you want to know?

Tags: comfort, family dynamics, mindfulness, nursing home

The Last Stop

We were really lucky. The nursing home where my parents spent the final stage of their lives is a good one, the best in the area I've been told, and I believe it. I would recommend it without a moment's hesitation. The building itself is well designed and homey; the residents are clean and well-tended. There are no unpleasant smelly-smells to bring to mind any bodily function. Staff members are compassionate and kind. There are lots of activities, parties and social events, but...

It's a nursing home. Even if you dress it up with a fancy name, it is what it is. It may be home-like, but let's face it; it isn't home. The many activities and contrived occasions (National Ice Cream Day! Luau Time! Strawberry Fest! Circus Week!) can at times feel forced, with staffers smiling a little too much. Sometimes, the sticky-sweet veneer can be jarring.

No amount of cheery seasonal decor can change the fact that, for the long-term residents, this is life's last stop. My mother, a dementia sufferer, mostly picked up on all the warm-fuzzy, happy-sappy attitude and became something of a smiling Zen master, living only in the moment, forgetting the past and unaware of the future. I would visit her, slapping on a happy face myself as I told her the same bits of family news over and over. I would tell her which of her grandchildren were in college, and which were still in high school. Yes, they were very busy. Yes, they got good grades. It filled the time.

If I had the emotional energy, we would reminisce about my childhood. Some days I had that energy; other times I just couldn't do it. We would always hug and hold hands. She always told me I looked just wonderful, a small silver lining and always an ego boost.

When I left, I would wave goodbye and step into the stairwell that was the shortcut exit. Sometimes I would catch my breath or choke back tears. Sometimes I just sat in the stairwell weeping. Eventually, I would pull myself together and walk out the door.

Once your parent is settled in a nursing home, your role as caregiver changes. Instead of doing laundry, you attend a care-plan meeting. Instead of helping with a bath, you check that she's clean and fresh. You touch base with the staff. You write checks. You fill out forms. You sign authorizations, which can seem weirdly like signing permission slips for a child. Maybe you join in activities; maybe you just visit.

It can be hard to step back and let others take over. It can also feel like a massive weight has been lifted off your shoulders. You may feel a complicated mix of guilt, sadness and relief. Whatever you're feeling is okay. For you, the adult child, the change can be emotionally unsettling, and why wouldn't it be? We want to believe, we need to believe, that this is the best place our parent could be. In reality, assuming that you've done your homework and found a good facility, it probably is.

Collectively as a society, we tend to give ourselves grief over nursing homes. We lament that previous generations all lived together, with children taking care of parents, all under one roof, and how awful it is that we "warehouse" our elderly. Let's take a step back and think about that a bit.

Step into an imaginary time machine and go back 100-plus years to the early days of the twentieth century. There are no antibiotics, so minor infections frequently claim lives. A heart attack is fatal. No bypass surgeries. A stroke or a broken hip? It's the end of the line. Lacking modern surgical techniques, a broken hip was a death sentence for an elderly person from 100 years ago. I recently uncovered the death certificate of my great-great grandmother. Cause of death? A broken hip. If she lived today, that hip would be set surgically, and she would be sent off to rehab and then maybe assisted living.

The big difference between the way things are now, and the way they were more than a century ago is that conditions that were death sentences then are treatable now. We have essentially lengthened the time between mom or dad being completely okay and independent, and their death. Now, instead of succumbing to a stroke or broken hip in a matter of weeks, our elderly parents can live for years in a state of dependence and disability. With good care, they can have a decent quality of life, but let's not kid ourselves. It's one thing to care for a dying loved one in our home for a week or two. It's something else entirely to care for a frail parent with multiple disabilities 24/7 for months or years on end. So let's drop the guilt trip over nursing homes, shall we? My mother thrived in a nursing home setting. She put on weight, and became sociable with the other residents who were as confused as she was. Overall, her last years there were good ones for her, even if they were a challenge for me.

A good nursing home will offer more than bare-minimum care. They have activities directors, and possibly volunteers, whose job it is to put a positive spin on what is realistically a fate no one ever wanted. The happy-face vibe may be appropriate for some residents, particularly those with dementia, but it can leave us caregivers feeling like we've fallen down the rabbit hole. How should we respond? It depends.

If your parent is like my mom, confused from dementia, the happy-face response may be the way to go. Dementia patients pick up on the mood around them. If it's happy, they are more likely to be happy too. If it's anxious, they will pick up on the negativity. On the other hand, if your parent is fully in possession of their mental faculties, the sticky-sweet happy approach may not be the best. Loving empathy grounded in reality may be the better path. What about anger? It's not uncommon for nursing home residents to lash out in anger, insist that they are just fine (even when they are obviously not) and demand to go home. A little emotional detachment and objectivity on the part of the caregiver is needed. It's easier said than done, but it may be necessary.

Nursing home life is new territory. Everything changes, for us and for our parent. For us caregivers, the experience can be emotional and at times, surreal. So be gentle with yourself. You're doing the best you can, and that is enough. Really.

Questions to consider:

- What are your feelings about nursing homes in general? Are those feelings rooted in your past experiences, society's stereotypes, or something else?
- If your parent is in a nursing home, ask the staff how they act when you are not around. Do they behave differently? How do you feel about it?
- If your parent had been in their present predicament a century ago, how might things have been different for them? 50 years ago? 25? Are they better off now than they would have been? What does this mean for you, their adult child?

Tags: dementia, encouragement, nursing home

Cough Drops and Hydraulic Lifts

Dad had been in the nursing home for about a month after moving from assisted living following the amputation of his foot due to diabetes, and it felt to me like he was becoming crankier by the minute. The leg was healing, and he felt well enough to start paying attention to his new normal. Compared to the assisted living area where he had spent the previous year, this was a prison: a posh, well-decorated prison, but still a prison. It was the final stop for him on his life's journey, and he knew it. Lashing out at the staff and at me was a very understandable reaction, but that knowledge didn't make it any easier to be on the receiving end of his moods.

Life is tightly regulated in a nursing home, and with good reason. Most residents are living with varying forms of dementia, and are mentally compromised. Many of the policies and procedures that annoyed my dad so much were for the safety of all the residents, but that is small comfort to someone used to relative freedom. This time, he wasn't allowed to keep any medications in his room for his own use, not even something as benign as a cough drop. He also wasn't allowed any of his beloved tools, not even a screwdriver to fix a loose hinge on his nightstand (something which, dammit, he could fix in 30 seconds if only they would let him).

Bath time was scheduled, and not always with his preferences in mind. Worse than that, sometimes it was delayed due to a situation with another resident. Dinner offered limited choices and was served too early. He also was at the mercy of the staff to move between his bed and his chair, a procedure that required two trained staff members and a hydraulic lift. Like a sack of potatoes, he was hoisted from one spot to another, in a procedure that saved the nurses backs, but wasn't exactly dignified for dad. On top of that, the coffee wasn't hot enough, they took too long to answer his buzzer, and the activities were geared toward ladies. Manicure day just wasn't his thing. The result? Frustration, complaints, and general grumpiness.

Who wouldn't be grumpy under such circumstances? Who wouldn't be stressed to have to listen to it all? Caregiving changes when a parent enters nursing care, but it doesn't end. Now, the task becomes making the best of what is, admittedly, the situation no one ever wanted. This is especially true for a loved one with intact mental faculties, who understands exactly what's happening and why.

Our first reaction is to slap on a cheerful smile, and to morph into Little Miss Sunshine, always cheery. Oh look, you get ice cream today! You like ice cream. They have a sing-a-long tonight! Doesn't that sound fun? We all do this to some degree I think, but it wears thin pretty fast with a cognitively intact parent. It's a guilt trip for them, and very draining for you. It takes an awful lot of energy to put on a happy face every time you walk through that door.

The root of the problem is that many things just can't be fixed. Rules are rules, and trying to argue or sweet talk the staff only rarely results in anything changing. No nurse's aide is going to risk his or her job by giving the diabetic in room 313 a candy bar when she asks for one. If you decide that the joy for your loved one from a small, technically off-limits pleasure is worth it, often the best you can hope for is that the powers that be look the other way. Sometimes they do. Sometimes they don't. In that case, prepare to face the music and explain yourself if need be. This is a job for you, not your loved one.

If your parent is cognitively intact, sometime it helps to just acknowledge the general crappy-ness of the situation. Forget the Pollyanna routine. Validate feelings instead: you're right, dad, it really sucks to be here. I'm sorry. I wish it didn't have to be this way. A little honesty and a shoulder to cry on can help. So can bringing in someone else for them to talk to and vent their feelings. A chaplain or counselor can share some of the load when it comes to listening to what feels like an endless lament, and can do so without all the emotional baggage that comes from being in a close relationship with the person who is unhappy.

What about you in all this? It helps to empathize and listen, but it can be very draining to endlessly listen to issues that you ultimately cannot change. If you can detach, even a little, it will help. This doesn't mean that you stop caring, or trying to do what you can to make things better. It does mean that you don't take on the burden of the impossible. It does mean that you know and respect the limits of what you can do, and don't allow yourself to slip into guilt over things that are, in the end, out of your control. There was no way I could stop the staff from using the undignified sack-of-potatoes hydraulic lift. For one thing, it wouldn't have been safe for dad to try to move him without it. For another, the strict rules and policies were bigger than my one situation, and would be followed even if I did rant and rave. The lift (pardon the bad pun) was not my burden to carry. It was beyond my control. So, even though dad still complained, I let it go and emotionally detached myself from the drama of it all.

When you leave from a particularly difficult visit, and walk out into the fresh air, take a few slow deep breaths, and imagine a big, dark blob sliding off your shoulders and onto the ground behind you as you step forward. Let that blob represent every little thing that is beyond your control, beyond your ability to change. Consciously leave it behind. Repeat the Serenity Prayer. Say some kind words to yourself. You are doing the best you can.

Next time you visit, put on a smile, but not a sticky-sweet fake smile. Validate whatever feelings your loved one has. Sympathize. Empathize. Do all those good things, but keep a little space in your own mind, a little place where you hold the thought that you, dear caregiver, are doing the best you can and that it's okay not to be able to do the impossible. As you leave, let the dark blob slide off your shoulders again one more time.

Questions to consider:

- Who validates YOU? Your feelings, your struggles? If no one comes immediately to mind, consider speaking with a counselor, minister, or other trained listener. It will do you good.
- If your parent is in a nursing home, even a good one, what aspects of it drive you nuts? How about your parent? Just venting a little can help.
- If you find yourself listening to a litany of complaints whenever you visit your parent, how can you consciously support yourself? How can you up the level of your own self-care to meet the stress you are facing?

Tags: anger, autonomy and control, nursing home, systems and structures

Dementia

The phone rang on an average afternoon. It was the nursing home. After an awkward apology for bothering me, the nurse explained that mom was agitated and they thought it might help if she could talk to me. Of course, I'd be happy to talk to her. No problem. They handed over the phone to mom.

Hi mom, what's up? I calmly greeted her, very much aware that my own mood could affect hers. Well, she was confused. Where was she? Why was she there? How long would she be there? Was I coming any time soon? She didn't know what was going on, she said.

Most of the time, mom just sort of went with the flow and was happily clueless at the nursing home, but not today. Every once in a while, without rhyme or reason, she would panic and become upset that she didn't understand anything. I calmly explained that this was where she lived now, and that she'd been there for months. Dad was nearby and would see her soon. It was all news to her. Fortunately, this particular moment happened at a good time for me, and I was able to drop everything and go to see her. I'll be there in ten minutes I told her. And I was.

I walked in and found her in her favorite chair in the common room, watching TV. Hi mom! She immediately smiled, and her face lit up with happy surprise. How great to see you! You look wonderful! Here, pull up a chair and let's visit. How are the kids?

And so it went. There was not a peep of anxiety in mom's voice, and of course she had absolutely no memory of our phone call that happened literally minutes before.

Welcome to the surreal world of life with dementia. It feels unsettling, like you've stepped into another universe, where up is down, the sky is yellow, the trees are blue, and like Alice in Wonderland, you never quite know what's around the next corner, or whether it will make any sense at all.

It's hard to see the inevitable changes that come with Alzheimer's type dementia on a day to day time scale. You may plod along seemingly in a holding pattern, but then something happens that jolts you into realizing just how much your parent has declined. Six months prior to the incident described above, my mother would have been able to hold the thought of being confused for maybe an hour, but now with the distraction of the television, it was gone in a matter of minutes, and by the time I arrived I was all psyched up for a non-existent crisis.

One of the mercies to you, the caregiver, of having your parent in a nursing home (as opposed to living with you) is that you are shielded, frankly, from most of the day-to-day endless loop of repeated questions and troubling behaviors that can quickly grate on your nerves like sandpaper on a sunburn.

Having a front row seat to watch someone you love mentally disintegrate before your eyes really hurts. Let's be honest. It is probably one of the most difficult things you will endure in your life, and it takes place in agonizing slow-motion over the course of years.

Every once in a while, I'll see a commercial on television for an Alzheimer's drug. These things always make me angry. They inevitably show a happy elder, and a loving adult child (or maybe spouse) caregiver with a beatific grin, offering a gentle hug or maybe a cup of coffee. Later, they take a walk together and smell the flowers. I want to shake my fist at the TV and yell this is bullshit!!

Alzheimer's and other dementias are ugly illnesses. They can rob your parent of not only memory, but also dignity. They can try your patience and push your buttons like nothing else. The following is a list of real-life situations. All were experienced either by me or other caregivers I've known.

- Parent wanders off, but luckily is found a mile away, dehydrated but okay.
- Parent refuses to eat; loses 20 pounds.
- Parent eats constantly because they forget that they've already eaten; puts on 50 pounds and becomes diabetic.
- Parent refuses to bathe for weeks.
- Parent will only wear one outfit, refusing to change.
- Parent refuses adult diapers, despite piles of feces on the floor.
- Parent screams and swears, becomes violent and strikes out physically.

- Parent sleeps all day, then stays up all night.
- Parent refuses to take any medication.
- Parent undresses in public.
- Parent believes adult child is spouse.
- Parent becomes frightened of "that old person watching me" when looking in the mirror.
- Parent forgets everyone, including family.
- Parent makes up demonstrably false "memories," insisting they are true.

Caregivers face situations like this every day, then still have to deal with the rest of their lives: their own marriages, families, jobs, health issues and stresses. Is it any wonder that sometimes we feel like we're hanging by a thread? The support of a good nursing home makes it a lot easier. The staff can emotionally detach in a way that you cannot, and the fact that they handle the bulk of the daily tasks means that you can focus on maintaining some semblance of a relationship with your parent even in the face of the decline. Here are a few ideas on how to do exactly that:

- If the facility has any outdoor courtyard or green space, take a walk together (or use a wheelchair). Do this after the staff helps your parent use the toilet. A side note: let the staff deal with toilet issues. It's their job, and one less emotionally fraught task for you to handle.

- Bring in a photo album from many years ago. Frequently, old photos can jog memories. Bear in mind that not all "memories" may be true. Just go with the flow and don't sweat the small stuff.
- Try offering a manicure, or a hand massage with scented lotion for some pampering.
- Listen to music together, especially music from your parent's youth.
- Read aloud to a non-verbal parent. Read favorite childhood stories, poetry, religious texts or an inspirational piece.
- If possible, share a meal, either in the dining room together or in your parent's room. Some facilities allow you to bring in food from outside depending on individual circumstances.
- If a meal isn't possible, maybe a treat? Share an ice cream, a piece of pie, or a box of candy (sugar free if necessary).

Most of all, realize that some days will be better than others. The more that you can simply accept the craziness of it all, the easier it will be for you. There will be some pretty awful days, but there will also be some good ones too. Savor the good, let go of the bad, and make extra effort to care for yourself even as you care for your parent.

Questions to consider:

- Are you afraid that you too will get dementia someday? What do you fear? What steps can you take now to minimize the chances of it happening later?
- Can you think of a metaphor to describe your experiences with your parent's dementia? Is it a roller coaster ride? Dinner on the Titanic? A parallel universe? Having a good metaphor for use in casual conversation can help those around you understand what you are going through.
- If your pre-dementia parent could travel through time and offer you some advice, what would it be?

Tags: anger, comfort, dementia, nursing home

Holidays Again

Dad had his foot amputated in early November, and had moved from assisted living to nursing care. It would be a permanent move, but he hadn't quite faced that reality just yet. Thanksgiving was coming soon, and then Christmas. Plans needed to be made, and fast. The previous year, we brought both of them to our house for the holidays. Last year, taking them out anywhere was a big deal, even for a short outing, but this year, the half-dozen steps to my front porch might as well have been Mt. Everest.

We decided to go to the nursing home Thanksgiving dinner, held early in the day. We would eat a light meal with them, then have a late home-cooked dinner at our house without them later. Both of my sons were home from college, and I wanted to cook, even if it did mean two dinners for us. The nursing home dinner was a well choreographed affair, with several assigned sitting times and fresh food brought out for each go-round. We ate in a large meeting room also used for church services with dozens of residents and their families, each trying to make the best of the situation.

It was...okay. The food was fine as institutional food goes, overcooked as is usual for residents who were used to soft, easily chewed fare. The biggest problem was that it just wasn't a family meal anymore. The nursing home kitchen just didn't use our family recipes. We ate. We visited. We took an awkward photo where dad looks rather distressed. We did the best we could.

For Christmas, we passed on the institutional dinner, instead opting to eat our traditional Christmas Eve feast, and afterwards to bring food for mom and dad so they could have it too, dining together after a short visit. We also had a longer visit with cookies and presents on the day itself. Like Thanksgiving, it was...okay. Not bad. Not awful. Not fantastic either. I think all of us were aware of the profound difference, and that the holidays would never be the same again.

In hindsight, this would turn out to be the last holiday season with my dad. We would have one more with mom, adapted and greatly simplified even from what I just described, but this year was rather strange. For me as a caregiver, it was neither here nor there. It was liminal.

Every family has holiday traditions, and as long as the older generation is present, the traditions seem to possess a continuity. Everyone gathers. Some people juggle time between various branches of extended family, trying to balance everybody's traditions. Kids are overfed and happy, then overtired and cranky. Elders oversee it all, usually from the most comfortable chairs in the house, watching the festivities with satisfaction.

All this changes when a parent enters nursing care. How to handle the new normal will depend on your unique situation. When presented with possibilities, I am generally in favor of the lower-stress option. No one in the family is well served by a tense, stressful, unpleasant holiday. Everyone's needs should factor in, including the needs of both the parent and the adult child caregiver.

There are two broad groups of permanent nursing home residents: those who are there because of physical limitations and those who are there because of cognitive limitations from dementia of various sorts. Of course, there's a lot of overlap between the two. The decisions you make about the holidays need to take into account which category is relevant for your parent.

The biggest question for holiday gatherings is where they take place: at the facility or outside of it in a family member's home. Many people naturally assert that OF COURSE they will bring their parent out for the holiday. What sort of awful person leaves their parent to spend a holiday in a nursing home?

If this is your first response, consider whom exactly are you worried about? Is it your parent or yourself? Are you worried about being seen as a "bad" son or daughter? Just sit with those questions a while, and be honest with yourself, even if the answers are uncomfortable.

There are three main categories of factors to consider when pondering what to do: physical limits, cognitive limits, and the needs of everybody else.

If your parent is in a nursing home for physical reasons, you need to consider how much activity they can handle. An hour? A half-day? Several days? Any outside visit, especially a day-long (or longer) trip to your home, will be a major disruption to your parent's normal routine. You will need to consider the physical nuts and bolts of a visit. Can you manage a wheelchair? What about toilet issues? Stairs? Is there a place where your parent could comfortably retreat from the hubbub to take a nap? What about dietary limits? Medications? Think carefully about the visit from the perspective of your parent, their personality, and their needs.

If your parent is in a nursing home because of dementia, you should still consider physical limits as well as cognitive ones. How easily do they tire? People with dementia thrive on routine, and any disruption of that routine may result in unexpected consequences and unusual behaviors like agitation or wandering. Would your parent recognize everyone present and be able to interact with them in a meaningful way? Would they recognize the house where the visit would take place? Elders with dementia may not even be aware that it even *is* Thanksgiving, for example. To them, it may just be another ordinary day, experienced fully in the present.

Finally, consider the rest of the family. Do you have guests from out of town? Are there young children present? Pets? How would the visit factor into the rest of the family's plans? Don't forget to consider your own needs and stress level too.

There is no right answer here. For some families, an hour visit at the nursing home may be just right for all concerned, including and especially the elderly parent. For others, bringing mom or dad out for the whole day may work. It all depends on the individual situation. Whatever you choose, you shouldn't make the choice based on guilt, or a rigid sense that we absolutely *must* do things the way we've always done them. Trying to maintain the holidays as they've always been is impossible. Things are changing. The perfect family holiday is an illusion. Expecting everything to be absolutely fantastic all the time is setting up everyone involved for a lot of disappointment. It is important is to realize that it's really okay to have a holiday that is just "okay."

Questions to consider:

- Have you ever made a decision based on guilt, or other's expectations of what you should do? How did it work out?
- Is there such a thing as a perfect holiday?
- How do your own childhood memories influence how you celebrate the holidays today? Is everything okay as it is, or is it time to make changes?

Tags: dementia, family dynamics, nursing home, rituals and traditions, through their eyes

Stages of Grief

It had gotten to the point that I dreaded answering the phone. Dad was not a happy camper, and boy did he let me know it. The coffee was lousy. The bananas weren't ripe enough. The phone confused him. He couldn't find the TV remote. And worst of all, the staff was a bunch of lazy bums. If they told him that his bath would be at 8:00, why the hell did they not show up until 8:15?? If they said, 8:00, it should be 8:00, dammit!! If he were in charge, things would be different...

Dad had moved from his assisted living apartment to the skilled nursing building in November after his foot amputation. It was a permanent move, and he knew it, even if we didn't really talk about it all that much. The upside was that now he got to share a room with mom and they were back together again. The downside was, well, everything else. For a man whose whole identity was tied up with the idea of being in charge of things, it was a tough blow.

A couple months later, I still dreaded answering the phone, but now instead of hearing the latest rant, I heard sobs. "It's all over," he lamented as he broke down in tears. This was frequently followed by, "Shit!" as he berated himself for losing control. More than once I dropped everything and went to him when he was like this. I didn't feel right about trying to put a rosy spin on the situation. Besides, it was getting harder and harder to find anything positive to say. So mostly I would just sit with him and hold his hand, or hug him and let him sob all over my shirt. Usually after about 15 minutes of this, he would beg my forgiveness, which was of course freely given without a moment's hesitation. He died peacefully about a month later.

Chances are you've heard of the Stages of Grief even if you're not familiar with Elisabeth Kubler-Ross, the Swiss-American psychologist who pioneered the concept in the late 1960s. The classic five stages are shock/denial, anger, bargaining, depression and finally acceptance. Not everyone experiences all the stages, and the order can vary along with the time spent in each stage. Sometimes people cycle back through previous stages as they grieve. Of course, there is no right or wrong way to grieve, but for many people, grief really does follow the stages. The thought of grief being a process that one eventually resolves (even if some lingering aspect of that grief remains for the long term) can be comforting, and the idea of the process having a structure of sorts can make it somehow less frightening.

Usually, when we think of the stages, it is in the context of grieving the loss of a loved one through death, but we can experience grief for other losses as well. In hindsight, I've come to realize that my dad experienced grief for his own decline and ultimate death with such textbook precision that he could have been Exhibit A for a psychology symposium.

At first, after his amputation, he was in shock for a week or so, and life just sort of happened *to* him. He was unusually passive. Next came anger, loud and clear with all the complaints and problems and endless phone calls. A little later, he latched onto the idea of a new wheelchair. Once he had that, everything would be okay again. Sounds like bargaining, doesn't it? When the wheelchair arrived and things didn't magically get better, the depression came, along with the second round of phone calls, this time laced with tears. Finally, a few days before he died, he calmly told me he loved me and to look after mom and my kids. I realized later that he had grieved his own decline and ultimate passing, and had reached a place of calm acceptance.

In the process of caring for your loved one, even before their passing, you may experience grief. It may follow the classic path, or it may be a less orderly process. We expect it. But what we may not expect is that our parent too, may grieve like my father did. For the elder, there is very important inner work to do: that of letting go and making peace with their life as it has been lived, and along with that comes grief. A loved one may grieve the loss of their home, spouse, friends, independence, driving, a hobby, a community, or anything that was a significant part of life as a younger person.

Your parent may move neatly through the stages, or get stuck in one for quite a long time. The process may be conscious or unconscious. As adult-child caregivers, it's helpful to understand the process and not sugarcoat their grief by trying to convince them that everything is just peachy-dandy. Trust me, if they are cognitively intact, they know better.

When your mother or father is grieving a loss, simply acknowledging the significance of that loss can be comforting. Just like us, our loved ones want to be heard and acknowledged. Even if we can't honestly say that we know just what they're going through (because we don't, really) we can offer affirmation that yes, this is a very difficult time. Eventually, the final stage of acceptance may come, and with it the gift of inner peace for the person doing the grieving.

It's hard to watch a loved one grieve for their own losses, even if it is a healthy and valuable process for them in the long run. When it's clear that grief in its various stages is at work in the psyche of our parent, we as caregivers need to step back and affirm the process. We need to resist the urge to try to fix everything, or gloss over the very real losses, or rush them through the stages. There is no such thing as a quick and easy way to the peace of acceptance.

I think there is such a thing as "good" grief. If we can experience our grief, integrate its lessons into our psyche, and grow in heart and spirit from it, then grief becomes a catalyst for living more fully and thoughtfully. We become more openhearted people. Our compassion for others and ourselves grows.

Looking back I can see that dad gave me a great gift. Reflecting on his experience helped me to become more conscious and aware of my own grieving process. At times like this, it is possible that our elderly loved one can be our teacher. There is a Buddhist saying that when the student is ready, the teacher will appear. Sometimes, our job as caregivers is simply to be ready.

Questions to consider:

- What losses have you grieved in your life so far? Did they follow any pattern?
- Has your parent exhibited any signs of grief for the losses of aging?
- What do you think "good" grief looks like?

Tags: anger, grief, mindfulness, nursing home, through their eyes

Goals, Paperwork, and Change

It was around 11 p.m. when the phone rang. Mom was having trouble breathing. They wanted to take her to the ER. No, I answered. What could they do to keep her comfortable right there? Put her on oxygen. Good. Do that. I'll be right out.

By this time, I knew what I didn't want for mom, who was now 86. I knew CPR would be a bad idea. She was a DNR (do not resuscitate). I knew she didn't want to ever be "hooked up to machines" (she had a living will). I knew we didn't want a lot of invasive tests. We had POLST orders on file to guide the staff. Yet, none of that was enough to fend off small daily crises, any one of which could have easily landed her in the hospital in spite of all our best pre-emptive paperwork efforts.

By the time I got to the nursing home, she was in her favorite chair, breathing oxygen from a portable tank, and cracking jokes. She was fine. She was not in distress. She was not in pain. Meds and extra oxygen had been enough to avert a few miserable days in the hospital.

At the next care-plan meeting a few days later, I asked for a hospice evaluation. She qualified, and was put on hospice services the following week. At that point, I breathed a sigh of relief. The chances of her landing in the ER against our wishes were significantly lower than just a few days earlier.

As caregiving progresses, the goals shift, medically speaking. Treatments and interventions that are suitable for a 72 year old might not be the right choice for that same person at age 85. It's good to stop now and then and think about the goals for your parent's care. The biggest question is whether the focus of care is on length of life or quality of life in the present. Imagine those two goals on a continuum, and think of where your parent is on that continuum.

At one end, the focus is on length of life, and your parent is cognitively intact and willing to tolerate discomfort in the present for the likelihood of extending life in the future. A good example of this is a bypass operation for an otherwise healthy 70 year old, who endures the surgery and a few months of rehab, emerging healthy and strong to live another decade or more. The other end of the continuum is where the focus is completely on comfort and quality of life in the moment. This might be suitable for a bedridden 90 year old with dementia, where decisions are made on a day to day or even hour to hour basis.

The messy stuff is, of course, in between. How much discomfort is tolerable? What is the potential benefit of a treatment or test? What are the chances of a full recovery? What is the goal? Consider both the physical and mental/cognitive state of your parent. Once my mother was on hospice care, we even refused blood tests. She didn't like needles, and to us, any small benefits simply weren't worth subjecting her to something she feared and hated.

There are always choices to be made, always tradeoffs to be had.

Usually clear black and white answers are few and far between. Keeping your goal in mind helps. At this point in my mother's life (age 86, with dementia, living in a nursing home) my goals were twofold: physical comfort and emotional well-being. That was all. If a treatment didn't contribute to either of those, we refused.

Of course, goals are great to guide you, the caregiver, but they are a challenge to implement in real life. The night I described was a weekend, and the staff on hand were substitutes, not the usual people, resulting in a situation where I needed to be physically present to make sure our wishes were followed. Don't just assume that because you've got all your paperwork in order (DNR, POLST, etc.) that your wishes will be followed when push comes to shove.

If your wishes and goals tend toward less intervention, you must speak up loudly and regularly to all who will listen. Your parent is particularly vulnerable on weekends, vacations and holidays, when the staff may include more substitutes and "floaters" who don't know you or your parent, and are liable to err on the side of intervention, especially if they are unable to contact you.

Hospice can help. With hospice care, the goal is clear to everyone: comfort. Treatments, medications, and interventions all serve that one goal and no other. In a nursing home setting, hospice workers assist and supplement the regular staff, but the biggest benefit is that your family's wishes are now crystal clear. If your parent is in distress, instead of a traumatic run to the ER, the hospice nurse is called.

For you, the caregiver, having hospice on board can reduce your stress level considerably, allowing you to relax into the present moment. No longer are you fighting the system or weighing one treatment against another. What matters is right here, right now.

There is a tendency towards only bringing in hospice care at the last moments of life. I urge you to consider it sooner rather than later if your family's goals for comfort care are clear. Having hospice on board sooner allows your parent to develop a relationship with the hospice nurses, aides, chaplains, etc... Trust can develop. Your parent's personal quirks and preferences can be learned by the nurses and integrated into care. A gentle rhythm can emerge as everyone settles in. Things quiet down, and an aura of calm and peace can grow.

For you, the caregiver, something shifts internally when hospice arrives. Your role once again has changed. Now, you are less of a vocal advocate and more of a companion on the way. If you opt for hospice in your parent's home outside of a nursing home setting, bear in mind that they do not provide live-in services. I suggest that you bring in someone to help with the day to day physical care. This could be family, friends, or paid help to allow you have enough energy to focus on your and your parent's emotional needs.

Allow yourself to experience this time as sacred, however you define that word, because it is. It really is.

Questions to consider:

- Have you given much thought to end of life care? What general impression do you have of hospice services?
- Where are you now on the continuum described above?
- Where were you six months ago? Have things changed? Where do you see your parent six months from now?

Tags: comfort, crisis, encouragement, mindfulness, nursing home, planning ahead, systems and structures

Hit the Pause Button

To this day, I'm not completely sure how he got there. Dad was mentally sharp but physically disabled. We had talked many times since his leg amputation about how he didn't want any more hospitalizations. He'd had enough, thank you very much. And yet, there he was. I had gotten the call when he was already en route to the hospital, too late to change things. He had a fever, they said. They wanted to admit him for observation. I shouldn't worry.

I had just talked to him the day before. The call was brief. I was getting over a nasty head cold, and my voice was nearly gone. He sounded fine. Everything seemed normal.

Ugh...here we go again. I thought to myself that he was going to be royally pissed. It was the middle of the night, and I knew the drill. We'd been down this road several times before: a day or two of observation, a few tests, maybe an IV, and he'd be released, mad as a hornet for missing an event like the monthly men's breakfast, where the food was especially good.

Still quite sick myself, I decided to sleep a couple more hours then go first thing in the early hours of the morning, when the doctors made their rounds. I arrived at about 7 a.m., coffee in hand, braced for a cranky dad, my voice still not fully recovered, expecting the usual, except...this time was not the usual.

This time he had been moved to the Intensive Care Unit. The fever had come from an infection that had spread to his bloodstream and suddenly gone septic. What did I want them to do? The prognosis was as bad as it could possibly be. Even with aggressive treatment, the likely outcome was not good. After several consults, I decided that he would be released back to the nursing home and go on hospice care the next day as soon as we could make the arrangements. It was a weekend, and things would take a little longer to sort out. In the meantime, they would keep him in the ICU for the day and stabilize him as best they could, with comfort as the first goal. I spent the rest of that day there in the ICU with the curtain pulled closed for some privacy, just sitting with him.

I look back on that day as a sacred time. Dad slipped in and out of consciousness. He held my hand. I held his. He spoke only a few words. Mostly, I just sat with him, watching him sleep, watching him breathe. I breathed with him. We were simply there together, and it was enough.

If you've been caregiving a while, it starts to become normal. Even in emergencies, you might feel like you've seen this movie before. The plot goes something like this: parent is short of breath, or has a fever, or just isn't right somehow. Off to the hospital you go. Hurry up and wait. Talk to Doctor A, Doctor B, and a whole alphabet soup of nurses, aides, social workers and therapists. Parent is treated, stabilized, given a new med and discharged. Repeat as needed. It feels like it will go on forever.

Of course it doesn't. One of those days will be the big one, *the one*, the time you knew would come eventually but not now, except that this time, "now" is really now. There is no preparing for this day. It happens when it happens.

When it does finally happen, it calls to you to drop everything and…Be. Here. Now. You may never get another chance. Call off work. Cancel everything. Inform only those who really need to know. Don't worry about the world. Hit the pause button on your life. Put your cell phone down, and only check it occasionally. Leave your social media behind.

This is not the time to argue. It's not the time to expect long, detailed answers, or deep discussions. Your parent's final days are a time when all the complexity of your relationship is distilled down to its most basic and essential foundation. It's a time to simply be present, fully present. Dr. Ira Byock, author and expert on palliative care suggests four simple responses: please forgive me, I forgive you, thank you, and I love you. Those four phrases encompass so much depth and richness in just a few words. I urge you to consider them.

Forgiveness can be especially delicate. You may ask for forgiveness and not receive it, or you may ask and your parent is physically incapable of responding. If in doubt, ask anyway. Say the words. More often we regret things we do not do more than things we do. Even if what you seek is not forthcoming, you can reach a state of peace knowing that you reached out and tried to reconcile.

If you are the one thinking about offering forgiveness, remember that it is as much about you as it is about your parent. Forgiveness doesn't mean that the wrong is forgotten or insignificant. It doesn't even mean that the person necessarily deserves to be forgiven. It means that you are letting go of the corrosive resentment that eats at your own soul. Thank you is a phrase that most adult children can say with sincerity. As adults, we begin to see our parents as human beings with struggles and flaws, who did their best even as they carried their own emotional history and baggage into their parenting. We can say thank you for doing your best or thank you for trying even if our relationship is complicated and fraught with difficulties.

I love you is at once the simplest and most profound thing we can say to a dying parent. Say it. Even if that love is imperfect, complicated or messy, it's still love. Say it, and keep saying it if you possibly can. Love offered freely is never wasted. If you can, spend some time in silence with your parent. Hold their hand, stroke their hair, kiss their cheek. Sit quietly with them, simply being together. You are two unique people, who share a deep connection. Spend some of that quiet time with some happy distant memories in your mind. Consider the passing of time, the nature of life, the meaning of love. Just be. Dying days are liminal, a sort of time-out-of-time when the busy-ness drops away, and we exist outside of our usual routines. We hit the pause button, slow down, and enter what can only be called sacred space and time. It may feel surreal, but in truth it's one of the most real things we will ever experience.

Questions to consider:

- Is there anything you would regret not saying to your parent?
- Is there anything you regret having said to your parent in the past?

Tags: at the hospital, comfort, crisis, mindfulness

Confronting the System

The day my father died was harder than it had to be, and that's really saying something. He was in intensive care, with an infection that had gone septic. Against his expressed wishes, he had been taken to the hospital a couple days earlier, and sent to the ICU. The prognosis was grave, but a plan was in place. He was to be released back to the nursing home on hospice care in the afternoon. I taught my classes for the day, and came home to have a bite of lunch before going back to the hospital.

The phone rang. It was one of the ICU nurses. I'd better get over there quick, she said. An overly eager young resident was keen to order more tests for dad despite our expressed wishes that he simply be kept comfortable until the details of the transfer could be worked out. The resident wouldn't accept the notes in the file or the word of the nurses that we didn't want any more interventions. If I didn't come myself and speak up, dad would have the tests whether we wanted them or not.

Off I went, leaving my lunch in the microwave, uneaten. I was furious. Grief and anger mixed and mingled in my weary heart, and it was all I could do to keep my voice steady as I walked into the ICU.

Why did they want to do the tests? Hadn't I signed papers? Hadn't we made our wishes clear? What's the problem? Well, they couldn't be sure. Sometimes families said one thing and wanted something else. Maybe the tests would give them more information.

I looked the resident squarely in the eye. "No. More. Tests. Is that clear? He is to be released to hospice care this afternoon. You are to do NOTHING except keep him as comfortable as possible. Is that clear enough for you or do you need me to say it again?"

"Well, okay... now that we've cleared that up..."

It was never unclear, not to me at least and not to the nurses who had tended him for the past two days. I needed fresh air. I stepped out into the cold February air, walked quickly to my car, got in and sobbed.

As I've said before, the system of health care for the elderly in the U.S. is not set up for thoughtful reflection on the quality of a loved one's life, or even a conscious consideration of the goals of care. The default goal of the health care system is to preserve life at all costs, and do anything and everything in service to that goal. That may be fine for a young accident victim, or a middle-aged cancer patient, but when it comes to our elderly parents, the default frequently does more harm than good.

We owe it to our loved ones to consider various end of life situations before we find ourselves standing in the ICU, sleep-deprived, trying to do the right thing but not really sure what that is, swept along by the defaults of the medical system. My father's prognosis was not good. With aggressive treatment, he may have lived a few more days or maybe even a week in the ICU, but at the heavy cost of much more suffering on his part, and the quality of that final week would have been very poor. The defaults of the system dictate that elders be given all the interventions that modern medicine can conjure, regardless of whether or not they are appropriate. We, as well-meaning family, want to feel as though we have done all that we could, and as a result frequently agree to the defaults only because we have not really thought them through to their logical end. Eventually, death comes whether we acknowledge it or not, and "fixing" all our parent's medical problems becomes a task akin to shoring up a sandcastle against the rising tide.

In my experience, most doctors and nurses are pleasantly surprised to find a family member who isn't looking for more treatment options in an essentially hopeless situation. They may be hesitant at first, but usually welcome a frank and open discussion of reality once they realize you, the adult child, are not hostile to it. Unfortunately, many doctors practice defensive medicine, since they realize that they are more likely to be sued for the tests and treatments they don't order than the ones they do. Your task when speaking to them is to get them to move past the defensive mindset. Added to the mix are younger doctors who may be eager to try out the latest techniques. At major research and teaching hospitals, the default may be even more heavily skewed towards high tech interventions simply because they are available.

It helps to consider *why* people (including you) might be drawn to more interventions, even when they accomplish little. Is it your parent’s clearly expressed wish? If that's the case, then follow their wishes. More often than not, though, it's us, the adult children, who go down the default path, for our own reasons. Maybe we have unfinished business with our loved one, and just aren't ready to let go. Maybe we feel guilt over issues long past, or wish we had been better sons and daughters. Maybe we harbor anger towards our parent, and unconsciously act on that anger.

If you have thought through your situation, and have a clear goal in mind, especially if that goal is minimal intervention and a focus on quality of life, talk to anyone who will listen, over and over, about those goals. Doctors need to hear them repeatedly, from you, to maximize the chances that things will go your way when the going gets tough. Talking about it frequently also helps you too. It helps you come to terms with the way things really are, and it helps build up your own inner strength that you may need if you ever find yourself needing to speak up and advocate for your parent.

Don't be afraid to ask questions. If you are inclined to "do all you can" for whatever reason, discuss with the doctors how patients like your parent fared with a given treatment. Was it successful? How is "success" defined? What would likely happen if you do nothing? If death is near, what options are available for comfort? Talk to doctors, but talk to nurses too. Often they have valuable insight that comes from being more closely involved with patient care that doctors just don't have. Take an hour and think before you make any decisions. When it's all over, years from now, you'll be glad you did.

Questions to consider:

- Has your parent expressed any end of life wishes to you?
- If not, and if they are unable to speak, ask yourself what would you want for yourself if you were them?
- Dig a little deeper into your own thoughts about end of life care for your parent. Are there any old patterns expressing themselves in your actions? Are they positive or negative?

Tags: anger, at the hospital, crisis, planning ahead, systems and structures

Intimate Strangers

Dad was dying. That much was clear. He had been released from the hospital after a brief visit to the ICU with an infection that had developed into sepsis. No one at the hospital seemed sure how much time he had left but they knew it wasn't much: two days, or maybe three? I wanted to make certain he was kept as comfortable as possible back in the nursing home, and had signed papers for hospice care.

He was back in familiar surroundings, in his own bed, when the hospice nurse came and told me he would likely die that same night, sooner than I had imagined. We made hurried phone calls, and brought my mother in to see him. Amazingly, despite her dementia, understood what was happening. She lovingly said her goodbyes. Later that same evening, she would forget all of it, but at that moment, it was the real thing.

Throughout that evening, as we kept vigil at his bedside, a hospice worker stayed with us. I'd never met her before. She was expecting a baby. We talked like old friends, about pregnancy, labor and delivery, her work with hospice, and my dad's life, all with him right there next to us. It felt somehow complete and fitting that the conversation flowed between these two poles of the new life yet to be born and the life that was ending in front of our eyes.

As time passed, the night shift nursing home staff brought us a cart of food and drinks. One came in to say goodbye to dad. Here was another person I'd never met, but she knew him. It was a little bit jarring, but in the end we shared a hug and I shed a few tears.

Throughout that evening, several strangers came and went from dad's bedside. Some knew him, some didn't. Each had a role to play as his life faded. He passed peacefully surrounded by family, with the intimate strangers kindly stepping back for the moment to give us space and time together to say goodbye.

Death is a profoundly intimate experience. If you are able to be with your parent at the hour of their death, you may find yourself sharing at least some of this life-changing time with complete strangers, and that's not a bad thing.

You may have had the experience of meeting someone on a plane or train, or some other situation where you are stuck together for a period of time, but know that after it's over, you will likely never see that person again. It's not uncommon to find that if you hit it off with that person, you suddenly share very private thoughts and experiences. You may open up in a way that you would never do with a friendly acquaintance in another setting.

It is similar, but much more emotionally charged, when one encounters strangers when a loved one is dying. I think this is especially true of hospice workers and nursing home staff, who attend to the dying, but who aren't as rushed as hospital nurses, and who also aren't as close to your parent as you are.

If you meet such intimate strangers as these, don't be afraid to open up, or shed a tear. It can be incredibly cathartic and emotionally healthy to do so. Hospice workers in particular are trained to be compassionate listeners, and can provide us with a safe space to vent or grieve.

The presence of clergy can be helpful too, especially if you are of the same faith. Most hospital chaplains are trained to be supportive to people of all faiths, or no faith at all. However, if a minister, priest or rabbi is employed by a religiously affiliated nursing home or hospital, he or she may or may not be comfortable outside the boundaries of the "official" faith. This may lead to awkward moments, especially if you are of a different faith, or are not religious at all. Much depends on the attitude and skills of the individual chaplain. Don't automatically assume that a chaplain of a differing faith will be unhelpful. You may be pleasantly surprised.

If, however, you find yourself in a religiously awkward situation, where someone (clergy or otherwise) is making you feel uncomfortable, don't hesitate to either #1 step out for some strategic fresh air yourself or #2 simply ask the person to leave. If you don't want to deal with #2 yourself, consider delegating it to a trusted friend, your spouse, or even another staff person with whom you feel comfortable. At such a profound time, you shouldn't have to put on a polite face to placate a "helpful" stranger.

If the awkwardness is caused by your sibling or other relative who has just as much cause to be present as you do, maybe take shifts to sit with your parent. You take an hour or two, and then let your sibling take over while you step out. Hospice workers or nursing home staff may be able to function as a buffer between stressed out siblings who aren't on the best of terms. Obviously, this isn't the ideal situation, but it's better than arguments at the deathbed. Communicate your own needs through a neutral party if necessary. Ideally, you should be surrounded only by those people (family, friends, or intimate strangers) with whom you feel affinity and connection.

Recognize that you are vulnerable, your emotions are raw, and you may be exhausted. You aren't at your best, and neither is the rest of your family. You all are grieving, each in his or her own way. Be gentle with yourself and with others to the extent you are able. If there's ever a time in life when it's really and truly okay to fall apart at the seams, this is it. Give yourself permission to feel what you feel, and be who you are. There is no wrong way to grieve.

I firmly believe that there is absolutely such a thing as a "good death." In my opinion, a good death is one where the dying person is physically comfortable, as free from pain as possible, and his or her wishes are honored as much as possible. The surroundings are relatively peaceful and calm, and the dying person experiences an atmosphere of love and compassion. Wherever that happens, however that happens is good.

Questions to consider:

- Have you ever been in the presence of a person when they died? What was the experience like?
- Do you think there is such a thing as a good death? How would you describe it?
- Have you ever had the experience of emotionally connecting with a stranger?

Tags: at the hospital, comfort, family dynamics, grief, nursing home

The Boyfriend

The day of dad's funeral was sunny and cold, a beautiful winter day, which was good since we had to drive two hours to get there. It was held in his church in the town where he lived nearly his entire life. It consisted of two visitation sessions with a break in between, followed by a service. In other words, it was a very long, very exhausting day. I drank lots of coffee and wore comfortable shoes.

The small parade of visitors consisted of extended family, members of dad's church, long-time friends, business acquaintances and the like. As is usually the case at funerals of elderly people, many of those who came to pay respects were themselves getting on in years. Quite a few were unknown to me. Most were sympathetic. A few were rude. One man in particular stood out from the crowd.

He approached me in the receiving line, and introduced himself. Apparently, he had gone to high school with my parents, and dated my mother for a while before she took up with my dad in her junior year. He was very sad for my loss of course, but was most interested in seeing if my mother would maybe like to reconnect and get together sometime because, you know, he remembered her with such fondness since he had dated her. Was she here, and if so, where? Was she taking a break in another room? Could he see her right now please?

When I told him that my mother was in a nursing home 100 miles away, suffering from dementia and physically unable to attend, he visibly deflated on the spot, like a balloon quickly losing its air. The light went out of his eyes, and he mumbled his condolences as he quickly moved on. It was by far the most surreal moment of the day.

Talking about it later with friends and family, I came to the conclusion that when you're 85, you can't afford the niceties of polite delay when hoping to rekindle a romance. I genuinely felt empathy for him when all was said and done. We all want love in our life.

Eventually, your caregiving days will come to an end, and you will likely find yourself at a funeral of some sort, shaking hands with people you may not even know. You'll repeat the same story over and over to all comers, and chronicle your parent's final days. You may cry, or not. You may be a bundle of emotion, or feel strangely detached from the whole affair. Whatever you feel, it's okay. There is no wrong way to do this.

Most people who show up to funerals are polite and kind. They express their sympathy, shake hands or hug, maybe say a prayer, and that's about it. A few, like my mom's old boyfriend, may express something beyond condolences.

Everyone comes to a funeral with an agenda, a reason for showing up. That agenda may simply be to show support and kindness to you, the son or daughter left behind. It may be to do the socially appropriate thing, out of a sense of obligation. It may be to fulfill a religious purpose. If the visitor had a genuine relationship with your parent (good or not so good), that agenda may be something more personal. It may be to seek closure or to say something that needs to be said. It may be a petty agenda, gathering gossip to report back to others. Or, it may be to reconnect, like the man who came searching for my mother.

Whether noble or petty, people come bringing their own issues and baggage that may have nothing to do with you. Old family feuds may rekindle. Old grievances may be aired. People may do or say things that leave you utterly dumbfounded, confused, upset or angry. They are attending to their own agenda, not yours.

You will get through the day a little easier if you can get the support you need. This may (or may not) be from your immediate family. If it is, that's wonderful. Lean on each other. If that's not possible, the next best thing is to have a friend who can stay close and offer ongoing support throughout the day. If that too is not possible, then you are tasked with caring for yourself. Pack yourself a care bag filled with things like tissues, cough drops, water, a snack, breath mints, worry beads, ibuprofen, a squishy stress ball, or whatever you feel might help. Take breaks. Step out for some fresh air. Find a private space somewhere and claim it. Care for yourself even as you comfort all those who are trying to comfort you.

If the traditions surrounding the funeral don't resonate with you, it creates a special challenge. Maybe you are carrying out your parent's wishes when you would have done things differently. Maybe you now follow a different religious tradition or none at all, and feel disconnected from the trappings of the service and all that surrounds it. Maybe your relationship with your family is less than ideal, and even being in their presence is a cause for stress. If this sounds familiar, realize that you have choices, even if you do find yourself stuck for the moment with something that just doesn't click for you.

There's no law that says you can't do something else on your own, in addition to the obligatory stuff. You have an agenda too, and it's every bit as valid as the agendas of the other people who show up at the funeral. Consider a small gathering with friends of your choosing, sharing memories and support for you, followed by a potluck. Or maybe something completely private is best: a solitary hike, with a pinch of your loved one's ashes placed beneath a tree as you read aloud something meaningful for you alone. You could even have another separate memorial service at a different place or time, with clergy or a celebrant of your own choosing, especially if the actual funeral is far from where you live now, and your own friends aren't able to attend. The important thing is to realize that funerals and memorials are for the living, not those who have passed, and should serve the needs of the living, and that you, dear one, are among the living.

Questions to consider:

- Has your parent pre-planned any aspects of their funeral? If so, do their wishes mesh with your own?
- How can you honor the memory of your parent in your own unique way, a way that supports you and helps you heal?
- How can you honor your own personal needs while respecting and honoring the needs of the rest of your family?

Tags: comfort, family dynamics, funerals, grief, healing after loss, rituals and traditions, self-care

The Parallel Universe

The night my dad died was a difficult one for my mother...until it wasn't. When we first brought him back from the hospital to the nursing home, we carefully explained the situation to mom. She spent the next several hours at his bedside. At first, she cried. Then she sat and held his hand lovingly. She was fully aware of reality, for a while at least. Gradually, as time passed, and various staff members came and went, and the conversation with the hospice workers took off on this tangent and that, mom's comprehension began to fade.

A couple hours into our vigil, she joked about how loudly dad was "snoring," not realizing that his labored breath was a sign that the end was close. A little later, an aide asked if she wanted to dress for bed. She was quite tired at this point, and asked if I minded if she changed. Of course not, I said. The aide took her into the bathroom, and after about 20 minutes, she emerged in her pajamas. She looked across the room, where dad was. The hospice worker was with him. We had stepped out to take a break. She looked at the aide and asked, "is that my husband?" The aide answered yes. She nodded, and went off to her own bed. Lights out, curtain closed, she slept peacefully through the rest of the night. By morning, dad was gone: physically gone, removed from the premises to the funeral home. She didn't seem to realize that he had ever been there in the room with her at all.

A few days later, I brought flowers from the funeral up to mom's floor, and we visited as usual. Nothing had changed from her perspective. From then on, when I would visit her, it was like entering a parallel universe. When we looked at old photos, she would talk about dad in the present tense. In that moment, dad was alive. Afterwards, as I stepped out into the chilly air, I would re-enter the world where dad was gone. For the next year, these two worlds existed side by side.

To tell or not to tell, that is the question. Just how much should you tell a parent with dementia? There may be many situations where you may face this question. Here are just a few: the death of a family member or close friend, serious medical news, the sale of the family home...or less significant, but still unpleasant news like a grandchild who got a bad grade, a fender-bender, or the death of a beloved pet?

Like so many other issues that arise when your parent has dementia, there is no one right way to handle this. What works for one family may not work for another, and that's okay. It may also be that adult siblings prefer to try different approaches. One of the very few silver linings of dementia is the built-in reset button of memory loss. If one approach fails miserably, you can always try another next time without your parent remembering the unpleasant episode.

The questions to ask yourself when considering what to say include issues like how distressing is the news? Could they comprehend it in a meaningful way? Do they have any memory of the people or situations involved? Do they have a right to know? I felt like my mother had the right to know her husband of over 60 years was dying, to give her a chance to say goodbye. To me, the risk of her being distressed was worth taking. She did get to say goodbye, even if she forgot about it later, and that was enough.

Once you've delivered the news, do you have to repeat it over and over, every time you visit? I don't think so. If I had told my mother every time I saw her that my dad had died, it would be as though she were hearing it for the first time. She would be hit with the shock, pain and fresh grief of that loss over and over again. What purpose would that serve for her? It would also bring with it lots of questions about the funeral, and why wasn't she told (even if she had been told)? Of course, *that* leads to discussions about memory loss, and before you know it, the conversation snowballs into an emotional ordeal for all concerned.

Sometimes the choice boils down to choosing the lesser of two evils: an emotionally upsetting conversation repeated over and over, OR the parallel universe experience where your parent remains mostly unaware while you carry the burden of understanding and knowledge. For me, the parallel universe was by far the better choice. Your mileage may vary.

Sometimes, depending on your parent's condition and level of cognition, you may choose to spill the beans, to let it out, and to cry together for just one day. Ultimately, there is no harm in that. You will have some catharsis, and your parent will retreat back into the blessed fog of not knowing. My mother never suffered deep lasting grief over the loss of her spouse. There is some comfort there I think.

If you choose the path of the parallel universe, to spare your parent pain, and to spare yourself the misery of having to break the news over and over, the hard part is that you, the adult child caregiver, has to bear it all. You know what happened, or is happening, and yet you can't open up to the very person with whom you would like to share the experience. So what do you do?

A time like this calls for taking your self-care to the next level. You are carrying a heavy burden. Make sure there is someone in your life with whom you can speak freely about whatever the situation is. This may be a sibling, your own spouse, a close friend or even a professional counselor or crisis hotline. Find someone to whom you can unload it all.

If you like to write, a journaling practice can be especially valuable. There are lots of variations here. You can go the traditional route of a notebook or bound blank book, or you can go more techie with an online blog. This doesn't have to be public. Many free blog platforms have privacy settings. You can create a blog that only you are allowed to read. If you want, you can unburden yourself on a few scraps of loose paper, then destroy it later on (burn, flush, tear in a million tiny pieces...). The point is that you find a way to unburden yourself on a regular basis as you walk back, again and again, into the parallel universe.

Questions to consider:

- Have you ever *not* told your parent something distressing that happened to you? What were the consequences, if any? Was it difficult to hold the secret?
- Have you ever told your parent something you later regretted?
- What do you do to let out your frustrations? If the answer is "nothing," how can you change that?

Tags: dementia, grief, healing after loss, self-care, stress, through their eyes

Late Night, No Regrets

When I visited mom in the afternoon, she seemed tired, but well. We talked, and she nodded off in her favorite chair. I sat with her for quietly. She woke up and we talked a little more, then I kissed her goodbye and said I'd be back in a day or two. I told her I loved her as I always did.

She had been on hospice care for a couple months by this time, for congestive heart failure. The goal was to keep her comfortable, and as importantly, to keep her in her familiar surroundings at the nursing home, in her favorite chair, and out of the hospital. She got regular visits from hospice nurses, but nothing that day was amiss. Nothing was out of the ordinary.

Later that night, a little after eleven o'clock, the phone rang. It was the nursing home. Mom was gone. She died peacefully in her sleep sometime around the shift change for the night staff. When they checked her at ten-thirty, she was peacefully sleeping. When the overnight staff checked her around eleven, she had died. They didn't know when.

We immediately threw on some clothes, and went out to see her, to be with her, to say goodbye. She was still warm. I kissed her cheek one last time. We sat with her for a while, and then walked out to our car into the chilly night air. As we drove off, it occurred to me that my caregiving days were over. My parents were both gone. My life would never be the same.

My mother's death was very different from my father's, described in the chapter *Intimate Strangers*. He died surrounded by family. She died alone. When I read that sentence, it sounds like a terrible thing, but it wasn't. She died peacefully in her sleep. It's not a bad way to go. If we're honest, it's something we might wish for ourselves.

When it comes to our aging parents, especially frail elders with various health issues, the truth is that we never really know when they will die. Of course, we don't know when we ourselves will die either, but we all unconsciously play the odds in our heads. When we drive off to work every morning, we operate under the assumption (nearly always correct) that our day will go as usual, and we will return home safe and sound. With our parents, when they are doing well physically, we operate under the assumption that today won't be "the" day. We have time. Lots of time. Months. Years maybe. Nothing will happen today. And for months or years, that's true.

Even when on hospice care, we have expectations. The nurses surely know what they are talking about. She's doing fine, they say, no reason to call the family from the far corners of the country. And most of the time, they are right. Except when they aren't. They are human too.

We know in the abstract that the day will come when our parents are gone, but when we are deep into the day-to-day slog of caregiving, that knowledge is very abstract indeed. One day it will be real, but not today...

Of all the various practices I discuss in this book, from planning ahead to managing stress, this one is probably the most important. Don't part with anger. Always leave with love.

Our elderly parents can really push our buttons. Especially if a parent has dementia, frustration and annoyance often runs high. That's normal! Completely, utterly normal. If you aren't snippy and cranky now and then, have your blood pressure checked! You're probably venting that frustration internally rather than out loud. Layered on top of a bad day at work, or a problem at home, dealing with our parents' problems is enough to tip us over the edge. We snap. They yell. We fume. They fuss. We throw up our hands in frustration, say things we regret later that night in the shower, and maybe shed a tear because we are just overwhelmed. It happens to us all.

I am not suggesting that you bottle up your emotions and work yourself into an ulcer and a heart attack. That's not realistic. I'm also not suggesting that you put on a sticky-sweet persona all the time. That's probably not possible! What I am suggesting is that when you part from your parent, even if you are not in the best mood, even if they are angry and yelling at you, even when both of you are at your worst, that you pause before you leave. Take a deep breath. Tell them that it's been a tough day all around, but that you still love them. If you possibly can, part on good terms.

Even if your relationship is rocky, part on the best terms you can muster that day. Of course, your best may vary from day to day.

That's okay. Just do the best you can on that day. Part without yelling. Part in peace if you possibly can. Then walk out and vent to your heart's content. Don't let your last words to them on any given visit be harsh ones.

This can be a challenging thing to do on a regular basis. It's really tempting, especially when you (or they) are in a really foul mood, to skip it just this once. Don't.

One of the best gifts you can ever give yourself is to know that you did right by your parents. You did your best: your imperfect, muddled, messy best. You absolutely don't have to be the perfect child. No way!! Your parent isn't the perfect parent either. Far from it. That's life. You will make mistakes in your caregiving. You will screw up. You will have regrets. You won't make the right decisions all the time. You won't be able to do all you might wish to do. That's okay. The trick is to have your regrets not be huge ones. You don't have to be the perfect child, or the perfect caregiver, but when they are gone, you want to be able to look yourself in the eye and know that you gave it your best shot, and it was good enough. In the end, it was pretty damn good.

One of the ways to make that happen is to get into the habit of never parting in anger, and always leaving with love. Just do it. You'll thank yourself later, when *that* day finally comes.

Questions to consider:

- Have you ever parted from someone in anger and regretted it later?
- Are you the type of person who carefully controls emotional expression, or are you very open with how you feel at any given moment? How does your personality affect how you approach the issue of parting in peace?
- What else might you do (for your own sake) to have few or no regrets when your parents eventually die?

Tags: anger, encouragement, planning ahead, stress

The Fellowship of Those Who Do What Must Be Done

Mom was gone, and there was work to be done. Phone the family. Call the funeral home. Make plans. Set the dates for the funeral. Make decisions. Order flowers. Empty the room.

When your parent dies in a nursing home, the bed is often needed ASAP for a new resident. We had 24 hours (not unusual) to clear out her things. At this point, mom's possessions had shrunk in volume enough to fit into her small room. She had clothes and toiletry items, her TV, a shelf, a dresser and nightstand from home, family photos and a few odd Christmas decorations in a box. We were able to fit it all into our minivan in one load.

Mom's funeral was much smaller and quieter than dad's (described in the chapter The Boyfriend). She died a year after him, and several people who came to his funeral had themselves passed in the intervening year. The fact that she had slowly disappeared from her social life as dementia took hold made a difference too.

Only a handful of people stayed for the memorial service, which we held at the funeral home itself for convenience sake. A few weeks later, only my husband and I were present with the minister as her ashes were interred together with my father in the church columbarium.

At that point, there was nothing left but the paperwork, which dragged on over the course of six months, despite the fact that mom's estate was tiny and uncomplicated. All of it sits in a box now, waiting for enough time to pass for me to consign it to the shredder.

It's been over a year now since mom died, and two years since dad left us. Every week, I still get junk mail addressed to them in my mailbox. Ironically, the most common item is advertising for life insurance. I also still get a subscription to Reader's Digest that dad had prepaid for nearly a decade. (I suspect he didn't quite realize that.) We'll be getting that, still addressed to her, for another two years. One thing I've realized is that time keeps flowing despite our losses and our grief. Life moves on. The sun rises, and the seasons turn. There is still beauty to be found in the world and in life. There always will be.

It can be jarring when a loved one dies, when you are busy doing the emotional work of raw grief, only to find yourself interrupted by all the many details that must be taken care of quickly. Even if your parent pre-planned their funeral (as mine did), there may still be lots of little things, surprising details that require you to pull yourself together enough to handle them.

There were several times in my caregiving years when I was forced to attend to the nuts and bolts of practical decisions even when I was in a state of emotional turmoil. It was at those moments when I felt like there ought to be some sort of society, with awards and certificates, "The Fellowship of Those Who Do What Must Be Done." I think there really is such a fellowship, an invisible one, populated in part by people like you and like me, newly orphaned caregivers who just step in and do the necessary work that the situation requires. These are the people who break the news to others, who repeat the same story over and over until their voice is raw, who arrange babysitters for the kids, who fill out newspaper obituary forms, who choose the color of the flowers, who pick out the hymns and readings... Imagine yourself getting your official membership in the Society. Imagine all the others who are in it with you, all over the world, just like you. Send them a mental shout-out of support. Imagine them sending one back to you. You may feel alone in your tasks, but really you aren't. Just knowing that can help.

In the middle of it all, don't forget to take care of yourself, especially if you are now the new "head" of the family, the one to whom everyone else unconsciously looks to for emotional support. Who is supporting you? As the dust settles, it's tempting to just jump back in to your daily routines, never missing a beat. Familiar routines can be comforting, and the feeling that things are getting back to normal (whatever that is) can feel reassuring, but nevertheless, you have endured a major life change.

Losing a parent, regardless of the circumstances or your relationship with them, is one of life's major inflection points, one that invites us to grow more deeply into the person we are becoming. It can take time for us to emotionally process the change, to integrate it into our psyche. Give yourself that time.

During the immediate aftermath, your life will be a flurry of sympathy cards and condolences from friends and colleagues.

Accept it all, and soak it in. Savor the shared memories, the kind words, and the hugs. Try to ignore the awkward or inappropriate comments that inevitably will come. Sometimes you can see it coming (maybe from that *one* neighbor or coworker who gets on your nerves) and sometimes it blindsides you. Realize that when your own grief is fresh, it is easy to find yourself more upset than usual. Comments that wouldn't bother you at other times seem particularly hurtful when grief is new. Just knowing this and being aware of it is helpful as you navigate the days following your parent's death.

Welcome to the Fellowship. Here's your membership card. You're one of us now. You'll be okay. You'll come out the other side of this hurricane, tired and wrung out, but still standing when all is said and done. You can do it. Really. Do what you have to do. Take care of yourself. Whatever you are feeling right now is okay. It will pass. There is no wrong way to muddle through the immediate aftermath of a parent's death. You are doing fine. Just keep breathing. Breathe in, breathe out. Repeat.

Questions to consider:

- Have you ever been on the receiving end of an inappropriate expression of sympathy or comfort?
- Have you ever found yourself at a loss as to what to say to someone who has suffered a significant loss or some serious bad news?
- How can you be extra gentle and extra kind to yourself when you are in extreme circumstances like the immediate aftermath of a death?

Tags: comfort, encouragement, funerals, grief, healing after loss, stress

Silence and Empty Spaces

Mom's funeral was over. The thank you notes were written. The flow of sympathy cards slowed to a trickle and eventually stopped. Her clothing had all been donated, and her few remaining possessions had been relocated to my house. Even the paperwork was nearly complete.

When dad died, I filled the gap by devoting more time and energy to mom. Now that mom was gone, it felt like empty space. In spite of the fact that my daughter was a very busy senior in high school, and we were deep into planning for her high school graduation and her older brother's college graduation, there was a sense of quiet, a silent place in my life where mom used to be.

I felt sad, but to my surprise, I wasn't overwhelmed with a tide of grief. Because of her dementia, I'd watched my mother slowly fade away for years. Somewhere along the way, she left me, though I couldn't exactly pinpoint when that was. Her physical passing felt almost like a formality of sorts, and I realized that I had grieved the loss of my mother for a very long time already. I had long wished that I would never experience a day when she no longer recognized me, and I got my wish.

I was very much aware of the milestones along the way for the first year after she died. Just like I did after dad's death, I kept a special journal, a place to write about my memories and the feelings of the moment as they arose. I also created a small memorial to her in my bedroom, with a few photos and personal items. Sometimes, I would light a candle there. After a year, I cleared the space and moved the photos to elsewhere in my house. I think of my parents often. The sense of empty space remains, but it isn't as intense as it was early on. I expect it will always be there.

One of the biggest adjustments you will likely make in your life is the transition from having living parents to being what some have called an "adult orphan." I've heard it said that you aren't really an adult until your parents die. There's a grain of truth there I think. The months after your last parent dies will be filled with little moments, unpredictable and random, where the reality of your new state will suddenly jump into your awareness, demanding your attention.

Grief is a path that we walk uniquely. For some, it is fraught with a roller-coaster of emotion, punctuated with tears. For others, it is a presence, a pervading sense of loss that slowly becomes bearable. However you experience it, remember that there is no wrong way to grieve. Some people follow the classic stages of grief in order; for others, the whole concept of stages is meaningless. If you find that after several months, you are consistently living with the same intensity of grief that you did early on, please, please do reach out for help. Grief is normal. Clinical depression is not. This is doubly true if you have a personal history of depression.

After all the hoopla surrounding the funeral is over, people around you will expect you to resume normal life even if you don't particularly feel ready. In Victorian times, a period of formal mourning was observed. Those in mourning would wear black, or some other visible, physical token of their grief, for a full year or more after the death of a loved one. This visible token was a signal to the world that the person had suffered a loss, and that a little extra kindness and understanding was in order. Although I wouldn't like to turn back the clock to the days of corsets and petticoats, I do think that society today is impoverished without some sort of public acknowledgment of mourning for a period beyond just a few weeks. Lacking a social tradition, we are left to our own devices.

You may find it comforting to mark a period of time (the first few months, or maybe the first year) with a ritual of your own. My memorial shelf allowed me to regularly acknowledge my loss to myself in a private way. It gave me a special place where I could just sit and remember if I felt the need to do so. My grief journal, which I wrote in at least once a week, gave me a place to work through all the emotions of those early days, especially milestones like her birthday or my first Christmas without her. Keeping up both of these practices for a full year really was helpful.

Here are a few ideas to spark your imagination. Pick and choose what resonates most deeply with you. If none of them do, that's okay too. Remember, there's no wrong way to grieve. I suggest a time frame anywhere from a month to a year, but as always, find what works for you. There are no rules.

- Keep a special journal.

- Create a memorial space in your home.
- Choose a piece of jewelry that belonged to your parent, and wear it every day.
- Read or reread your parent's favorite book.
- Set aside a regular time and listen to your parent's favorite music.
- If your parent had a favorite restaurant, go there regularly, intentionally, for a period of several months.
- Go to an in-person grief support group.
- Find a support group online and participate regularly for a set period of time.
- If possible, tend the grave. Plant flowers and/or put out seasonal decorations.
- If you don't want a full-blown memorial space with photos and memorabilia in your home, consider a simple memorial candle. Light it every evening.
- If your parent was religious, consider honoring their faith whether or not you practice it personally. Are there any traditions associated with mourning?
- Create a digital memorial, such as a blog or web page. Upload photos, or share memories with friends there.

Ultimately, the point of all of these actions is to support and comfort you, the adult child, through the most intense time of grief after the loss of your parent. You aren't obligated to do any of them if that isn't your style, but you should feel free to pick and choose any that bring comfort. Our society doesn't handle death very well. We worship fleeting youth, and deny the reality of aging and death. I truly believe we would be better served to value all stages of life, and the unique gifts they bring.

After the first year, then what? I'll repeat myself and say again that if your grief feels fresh and raw after a full year, get help, especially if you have experienced depression in the past. You should be feeling better after a year. If you aren't, that's a red flag and a signal to reach out. Eventually, grief becomes like an old injury: achy now and then, but tolerable. It won't ever completely go away, but it should get a lot easier to bear. You may decide to continue an annual remembrance of some sort, perhaps on your parent's birthday or another personally meaningful time. People of Mexican heritage observe *Dios de los Muertos* (Day of the Dead). Some Christian churches observe All Saints Day and conduct memorial services at that time.

Whatever you choose to do, know that your memories and experiences as a caregiver of your elderly parent have become part of who you are for the rest of your life. You aren't the same person anymore. You're all grown up now. Really.

Questions to consider:

- What unique aspect of your parent's personality might serve as inspiration for you going forward? Is there a way you can integrate it into your life?
- How have you changed as a result of your caregiving years? In what ways are you a different person?
- Do you agree with the assertion that only with the death of your parents do you truly become an adult? Why or why not?

Tags: comfort, funerals, grief, healing after loss, rituals and traditions

Through a Glass Darkly

It's been several years now, and my parents are still gone. Every now and then I have to remind myself of that fact. Photos of them decorate my house. Memories of them decorate my thoughts. My own children are moving into adulthood at college and beyond. Life moves on. Time keeps on flowing.

I have no clever story with which to begin this final chapter; that story has yet to be written. I catch glimpses of it, fuzzy and inchoate, or as the verse says, through a glass darkly: my own aging and mortality. At some point in our caregiving years, it hits us. We too will age and die. When we are children, we tend to live in that world of magical thinking where death is vague, something that happens to other people, to old people, never to us. As we venture out into our lives as young adults, perhaps a tragic death of one of our peers touch our lives. Maybe it was an accident, maybe cancer, or worse, maybe a suicide which is by far the most tragic of all. Suddenly, we realize that we too are mortal, that death can happen to one of us, even at a young age. Soon enough though, we are back to the business and busy-ness of our own lives, only to come home one day and realize that our parents are looking a lot older than we remember.

Time passes. Life happens. We build careers, and have families of our own. Then our parents need us. The parents we remember from our childhood have changed. They are weaker than we recall, frail even, and then they die, and we are left looking in the mirror at our own faces. We notice the lines, and the grey hair. Oh my god, we think. We are next. Even if we are in our 40s or 50s when our parents die, even if we have decades ahead of us, there's something profound to realize that the generational buffer between our own deaths and ourselves has disappeared. This is especially true when the last relative of your parent's generation dies. It may be an aunt or uncle, or maybe your parent is the last. Now, we are the elder generation, the keeper of the family stories, memories, and traditions.

As we watch our parents decline before our eyes, we cannot help but think about our own future. What will become of us? I think that's a completely normal worry, and one that we can actively take steps to address. My dad never met a bacon cheeseburger that he didn't like. He paid for that habit with a bypass operation. I can try to eat a better diet (and I do), and hopefully I can avoid his fate. Our parents' fate, whatever that turned out to be, doesn't necessarily have to be our own. We do share genes, but we alone are in charge of our choices and habits, for better or worse. So yes, do all that. Work on your cholesterol level. Exercise. Eat kale. Drink red wine. You'll die eventually, but hopefully the years in between now and then will be mostly healthy ones.

I have come to believe that our parents' aging and death offers us a priceless gift if we can recognize it for what it is. With their passing, our parents give us the gift of true freedom to grow into full and complete adults in our own right. With our parents gone, we can really, truly, at long last, grow up. We can be and become our true selves. Whatever faults your parents had, whatever collective family baggage they inherited and carried, whatever guilt they laid on you...it's over. You don't have to worry about dad questioning your financial choices, or mom asking why you thought *that* color looked good on you. Our parents were far from perfect. All parents are far from perfect. They tried their best, given the realities of their own lives, and as we became adults ourselves, we realized that, and hopefully were able to let go of old resentments. But after they die, it's different. Something shifts inside us, and if we can recognize it as a gift, we can step into our own autonomy, fully and completely. We're the adults now. Whatever our lives will be, it's on us. We are the captains of our own ship from here on out. Will we stay the course or chart a new one?

Since my parents' deaths, I find that I have become more outspoken and less self-censored. I find that I don't have to explain myself to anyone (maybe I never did, but it took them dying for me to realize it). I also find that, especially as an only child, I am very much aware of my role as the caretaker of the family stories, as well as the keeper of the family treasures. I want my children, and someday their children, to understand a little about the generations that came before them, to realize that all our lives are built on a foundation laid by those whom we never knew personally, but whose lives impact our own.

I have moments of sadness still, but I am not a puddle of fresh grief. I think of my parents, remember them with love, and thank them mentally for all they did for me. Life really does go on, and I want to truly be present for it, to soak it in, to experience all it has for me. It won't last forever, but then again, nothing does. Life, however long it lasts, is precious.

Losing one's parents is a wake-up call. As the poet Mary Oliver says, what will you do with your one wild and precious life? What will you do? Who will you be? What changes do you want to make? What qualities do you want to cultivate in your own soul? Where do you go from here?

Take your time and think deeply all these questions, but don't take forever. You don't have forever. Don't slip back unconsciously into whatever old rut this experience threw you out of. Or not...maybe it isn't a rut at all, but a well-loved path. The point is that you, the full-fledged, 100% grown up adult make that choice for yourself. It's the choosing that matters, the conscious and mindful inhabiting of your own life, fully. Now take a deep breath, and go out and seize the day.

Chapter Index with Tags

Digging the Roses: encouragement, family dynamics, healing after loss, moving

Diplomacy: autonomy and control, comfort, nursing home, systems and structures, through their eyes

The Endless Parade: autonomy and control, family dynamics, systems and structures

The Fellowship of Those Who Do What Must Be Done: comfort, encouragement, funerals, grief, healing after loss, stress

Finding the Humor: comfort, dementia, encouragement

Finishing the Pepper: comfort, healing after loss, mindfulness, rituals and traditions, self-care

Goals, Paperwork and Change: comfort, crisis, encouragement, mindfulness, nursing home, planning ahead, systems and structures

Hit the Pause Button: at the hospital, comfort, crisis, mindfulness

Holidays: dementia, mindfulness, stress

Holidays Again: dementia, family dynamics, nursing home, rituals and traditions, through their eyes

The Ice Cream Project: comfort, family dynamics, mindfulness, nursing home

"I need a connection": comfort, crisis, nursing home, self-care

Intimate Strangers: at the hospital, comfort, family dynamics, grief, nursing home

It is Imperfect: autonomy and control, rituals and traditions, self-care, stress

The Last Stop: dementia, encouragement, nursing home

Late Night, No Regrets: anger, encouragement, planning ahead, stress

The Muffin Incident: dementia, denial

Out of the Blue: at the hospital, crisis, planning ahead, self-care, stress

The Parallel Universe: dementia, grief, healing after loss, self-care, stress, through their eyes

Parent or Child?: autonomy and control, family dynamics, grief

Promises and Fantasies: autonomy and control, denial, planning ahead, self-care

Releasing the Past: family dynamics, mindfulness, moving, rituals and traditions, self-care

Rotten Potatoes and Other Unpleasantries: dementia, denial, planning ahead, rituals and traditions, self-care

Silence and Empty Spaces: comfort, funerals, grief, healing after loss, rituals and traditions

Sloppy Grief: dementia, grief, nursing home

Stages of Grief: anger, grief, mindfulness, nursing home, through their eyes

Stories from the Neighbors: autonomy and control, denial, planning ahead, through their eyes

The Stuff of Life: autonomy and control, family dynamics, mindfulness, moving

Suddenly Caregiving: crisis, encouragement, planning ahead
The Tale of the Table: moving, self-care, stress

The Thread Snaps: at the hospital, crisis, nursing home, planning ahead, systems and structures

Who is This Person?: comfort, dementia, encouragement, grief, through their eyes

Tag Index with Chapters

Grief: *The Boyfriend; The Fellowship of Those Who Do What Must Be Done; Intimate Strangers; The Parallel Universe; Parent or Child?; Silence and Empty Spaces; Sloppy Grief; Stages of Grief; Who is This Person?*

Healing after Loss: *The Boyfriend; Digging the Roses; The Fellowship of Those Who Do What Must Be Done; Finishing the Pepper; The Parallel Universe; Silence and Empty Spaces*

Mindfulness: *Black Sheep and Golden Children; Finishing the Pepper; Goals Paperwork and Change; Hit the Pause Button; Holidays; The Ice Cream Project; Releasing the Past; Stages of Grief; The Stuff of Life*

Moving: *Big Changes; The Conversation; Digging the Roses; Releasing the Past; The Stuff of Life; The Tale of the Table*

Nursing Home: *Big Changes; Cough Drops and Hydraulic Lifts; Dementia; Diplomacy; Goals, Paperwork, and Change; Holidays Again; The Ice Cream Project; "I need a connection"; Intimate Strangers; The Last Stop; Sloppy Grief; Stages of Grief; The Thread Snaps*

Through Their Eyes*:* *The Conversation; Diplomacy; Holidays Again; The Parallel Universe; Stages of Grief; Stories from the Neighbors; Who is This Person?*

For Further Reading

The resources listed below are ones that I personally used and found helpful during my caregiving years. They are only a small sampling of the many available for caregivers, and a good starting point for your research. I encourage you to search and read widely, and to seek out other caregivers for support and encouragement.

AARP Home and Family Caregiving Information:
http://www.aarp.org/home-family/caregiving/

The Alzheimer's Association (alz.org) offers information as well as message boards for caregivers to support each other.

National Academy of Elder Law Attorneys (NAELA), www.naela.org

Brackey, Jolene: **Creating Moments of Joy for the Person with Alzheimer's or Dementia: A Journal for Caregivers,** *Purdue University Press, 2008.*

Byock, Ira: **Dying Well: Peace and Possibilities at the End of Life,** *Riverhead Books, 1998.*

Dunn, Hank: **Hard Choices for Loving People: CPR, Artificial Feeding, Comfort Care, and the Patient with a Life-Threatening Illness,** *A&A Publishers, 2009.*

Gawande, Atul: **Being Mortal: Medicine and What Matters in the End,** *Metropolitan Books, 2014.*

Gross, Jane: **A Bittersweet Season: Caring for Our Aging Parents and Ourselves,** *Vintage Books, 2012.*

Kubler-Ross, Elisabeth: **On Death and Dying,** *Simon & Schuster, 1969.*

Mace, Nancy: **The 36-Hour Day: A Family Guide to Caring for People Who Have Alzheimer Disease, Related Dementias, and Memory Loss ,** *Johns Hopkins Press, 2012.*

McCullough, Dennis: **My Mother, Your Mother: Embracing "Slow Medicine" the Compassionate Approach to Caring for your Aging Loved Ones_,** *Harper Perennial, 2009.*

Acknowledgements

It is impossible for me to thank every single person who helped both my parents and me during my caregiving years and ultimately contributed to the writing of this book, but I will try.

Firstly, thank you to my family: my husband Patrick and my children Steven, Matthew and Julia. I would not have survived without your love and support. Thank you to my "sister from another mother," Rebecca Humphrey, who countless times without fail, provided exactly what I needed at the moment I needed it.

Thank you to my friends and colleagues at Thiel College who filled in for me when I was called off on one emergency or another. Thanks to my extended family: Alan and Ellen Fleissner, Chris and Lisa Fleissner and Gloria Weber for kindness, support and practical help with caregiving over the years.

Thank you to Rev. Karen Stevenson and Rev. Carmen Emerson for wisdom, compassion and simply being there. Many thanks to Dr. Christa Malinak for her excellent medical care and problem-solving creativity.

Special thanks to the administration and staff of St. Paul Homes in Greenville PA, notably the staff of the Heritage and Springs B. Thank you especially to the personal care assistants and aides who brought dignity to the hands-on tasks of caregiving. You all are exceptional people, professional and kind, and I will be forever grateful. I must personally acknowledge Sheila Wasser, social worker extraordinaire, for being the awesome person she is. Finally, I want to extend my gratitude to my friends and neighbors, to online friends from the Alzheimer's Caregivers Discussion Boards (especially Grassflower), and to the many nurses who listened. To paraphrase a famous saying, it takes a village to care for an elder.

About the Author

Rebecca James Hecking has a diverse and eclectic educational and professional background. She holds a B.S. in chemistry and an M.A./I.S. in cultural/equity studies. She currently teaches mathematics at Thiel College in Greenville, Pennsylvania.

She is the author of *The Sustainable Soul: Eco-Spiritual Reflections and Practices* (Skinner House, 2011) and has written for numerous online and print publications on lifestyle, inspirational and ecological topics.

She and her husband Patrick are parents to three young adult children who never cease to make their parents absurdly proud and ridiculously happy. They reside in Greenville where they are dutiful servants to their three feline overlords.